CW00338522

Fashion *after* Fifty

First published in the UK by Masquerade Editions
in 2008.

ISBN 978-0-9558623-0-4

Printed in Germany

Fashion *after* Fifty

Kaaren Hale & Felice Hodges

Masquerade Editions

Contents

Foreword

We have arrived at last: all grown up, wiser, full of experience and our own tastes. We may or may not have always been comfortable in ourselves but at this point we should be. We are a generation of doers. We have been educated and moved forward by events. We have campaigned for our rights and have pushed baby prams. We have had big jobs, paid or unpaid, we have raised money for good causes, sat on school boards, wined, dined, done the corporate thing and lunched with pals till we nearly dropped. We have raised children; some of us have helped raise grandchildren. We are good-looking, have exercised regularly and are far younger than our mothers were at the same age.

Who of us has not pulled out the family album and gazed in wonder at those old women of fifty and beyond, who seem so mature with their thick bodies in staid clothes. In comparison, we seem so much younger now. This might at first appear to be a generational delusion, but today we are in fact healthier, destined to live longer as a result of scientific advances from birth control to hormone replacement. We are the product of the conservative Fifties, the swinging Sixties, the boom-boom Eighties and sober Nineties. We have enjoyed many heydays, and few of us are ready to give up just yet.

So why is it that the fashion industry, with few exceptions, directs all its ideas toward the very young, or worse, toward the very boring? We are here, and we have hard cash.

Ask any friend. Do you like shopping these days? The answer is a universal "no": it is exhausting and frustrating.

There are no sizes. Everything is expensive and sold at the wrong season – just when you desperately need something, it has been out of stock for a month. Even those who enjoy fashion and the interminable search for a treasure to wear to a special event need an update on how to understand and cope with the rules of this difficult, challenging industry. Fashion should deliver pleasure, instead it is pain.

The trouble with being over fifty is everything starts to change. By sixty gravity has started to pull hard and by seventy there is an urgent need to cover up some of the wobbly bits. The female ageing process has not been helped by society's worship of youth and airbrushed beauty. This is a war of attrition. As Bette Davis once noted, "Ageing isn't for sissies." It is a bumpy ride.

But we need not give up. Although the lack of style mentors and fashion choices is disheartening, we do not have to fill our wardrobes with dreary clothes, insensitive to the high-spirited girl inside us who still craves fashion adventure. No more high heels just because you have hit sixty-five? If your balance is a bit less steady, go for a lower stiletto and carry on! Despite the youth-obsessed society of which the fashion industry is only one reflection, we continue to need to feel good about ourselves, to nurture our self-confidence, to re-educate ourselves about what works and why, to seek new doyennes of style and to retain beauty that is attainable past the first blush of youth.

Remember the angst that Hillary Clinton underwent as the fashion world repeatedly restyled her, with hairstyles and colours changing as often as Bill's taste in interns. She went blonder, pinker, blacker, bluer, more patterned and after a great deal of effort eventually found a fashion persona that worked. She now wears trousers to camouflage her less than perfect legs and an open neck white shirt to frame her face and neck. Her hair is a good medium-blond colour in a flattering cut. No more hair-bands, no more calf-length tweed suits.

We may not have Donna Karan to guide us personally through the minefield of middle age, but we can learn from our peers who already know how to do it, and enjoy the ride. This is a book about us, for a generation of women that has done it all, seen it all and still wants to look good.

Who Am I?
What Do I Want to be
Today or Tomorrow?
How Do I Get the Look I Want?

The world is hung up on celebrities. They are everywhere, selling everything from toilet paper to themselves. Whereas in our mother's generation models and actresses might have provided inspiration, today for the most part, they give us very little. So how do we know what we are looking for?

Although they have some common age-specific problems and needs, middle-aged women come in all shapes and sizes, just like their younger sisters and daughters. They are individuals who want individual fashions: tall ladies may want to appear feminine and girly; short women may have big appetites, personalities and stature; heavy-set women may be flirtatious and light on their feet; slim size sixes can be butch or sexless – "Ça depend," say the French.

We have identified some prototypes. You may find that you fall definitively into one category or perhaps into several. Knowing who you are or who you think you are, or who you would really like to be now, in your grown-up manifestation, will lead you to getting your style right. This is about evolution, and you are still evolving.

Still Rebellious After All These Years

You refuse to conform, always the first with the latest and most outrageous styles. You wore Comme des Garçons three-legged trousers just for fun and a pink mohair sweater down to your knees. This was amusing and liberating once but would be a bit sad now. For mature women there is still an entire world of fashion thinkers who can satisfy your rebellion against conformity, without making you appear ridiculous. Issey Miyake and Yohji Yamamoto, just two of the senior figures of the Anglo-Japanese scene, are still producing beautifully conceived, wearable and original clothing for women of a certain sensibility. One of their pieces can work wonders with a simple pair of trousers or a skirt. Pieces by Dries van Noten, Anne Demeulemeester, Sonia Rykiel, Rick Owens, Marni, Etro and Helmut Lang are also worth a serious look, and there is so much scope for originality simply by choosing a few key pieces from their collections.

Sizes can be a problem with the Belgian designers, but not with the Japanese. Their humanistic approach to women accommodates all shapes and ages. Indeed, their styles often look better on larger, older women. These clothes complement individuality and experience. The rebel has the character to carry them off.

However, try to resist doing the whole look, top to toe. Buy one interesting garment and make it a feature, not a costume. This can be difficult to deal with in department stores because the staff often have no clue how to display the pieces. Seek out smaller shops and boutiques (like Brown's or Matches in London, for example) to help you understand the look. Play with it to make it your own. Ask to see the "look book," which will show the catwalk models in full regalia. Research, experiment and do not be rushed.

Even if you are the rebellious type, the adult woman should still try to lengthen her body line, and quirky boots and high-heeled shoes can make a difference. Stay away from sports trainers but if you must wear them choose more elegant versions in leather and suede, which offer comfort and a bit of edge, like those made by Prada, Sergio Rossi, Camper, Tod's, Mui Mui and Puma. Top Shop in London is a trial for anyone with a noise sensitivity or aversion to crowds, but they sell some cheap and cheerful shoes to satisfy any foot fetish.

Classically Elegant Like Your Mother
Do you love the 1950s? Do you long for suits, cocktail dresses, tailored coats, dressing gowns and floating caftans à la Zsa Zsa Gabor? This was a glamourous look once and can be again, but it must be adjusted for the style of the day or it will appear dated. So many designers are once again creating distillations of this elegant and womanly style, but much of it is simply too retro, which is fine for young girls because for them it is new. You, however, must deconstruct this look and update it with hip, modern touches. There are plenty of designers to choose from: at the top end, Chanel, Celine, Caroline Charles, Dolce & Gabbana, Prada, Jil Sander, Brioni, Loro Piana, Jean Muir and Escada (to name a few); in the

middle range, Moschino Cheap and Chic, Sport Max, L.K. Bennett, Jaegar, Phase Eight and Hobb's; at the low end, H & M, Zara, Wallis and Top Shop.

We love the look of a plain grey flannel suit with a fabulous coloured shawl with furry fringed ends, a big 1940s brooch from Butler and Wilson (fake) or Peter Edwards (real), pea-green snakeskin shoes and an orange leather handbag. We love a beige tweed skirt with a matching twin set, a bib of coloured crystal beads and a short trench coat tied tight with a belt. Carry a bright blue leather bag, and go bare-legged if you dare! Mummy would not have risked it and *that* is the point!

Wear anything trimmed with fur, but not a fur coat. Wear garnets, citrines and aquamarines instead of diamonds. Go a little shorter or longer in the skirt, depending on your opinion of your ankles. Wear a brighter coloured lipstick and gloves – but they should be orange or green, not black or beige. Forget the pussy-cat bow forever! If you are attached to the idea of wearing a tea gown or floaty caftan for cocktails, hurry over to Allegra Hicks, Liza Bruce or any ethnic shop you see. There are specialists in the gauzy and flimsy everywhere.

Intellectual without Blue-Stockings (You are not a Prude)
This look is tweedy, subdued and conservative, but with a fashion twist or two can be brought up to date. You want to be taken seriously, but at the same time you want to project your femininity. You may be wearing Calvin Klein or Armani trousers and a man-tailored jacket, but underneath you have a silk embroidered camisole in a girly pastel shade, barely showing. You wear grey, well-cut trousers, a matching polo-neck, a skinny lizard belt at the hip-line and a loose camel-hair jacket by Zoran. You accessorize with woven, Cuban-heeled boots, amber or jet beads, antique ivory and tiny gold-drop earrings.

Your fashion cues come from museum curators, Woody Allen's heroines and university lecturers. Your clothes are statements of your intellectual prowess as well as your good looks. Black is worn always, and you especially love all the earth colours. Tobacco, saffron and taupe have a soothing and calming effect and are environmentally friendly. You can find what you crave at Jil Sander, Ralph Lauren, Strenesse, Margaret Howell, Krizia, Shirin Guild and Aquascutum. This is not cheap dressing.

Working Women Who Multitask: the Sandwich Generation (dealing with grown-up children, husbands and ageing parents all at the same time)
Working women have the most complicated sartorial lives of all. There is a certain uniform associated with many professional occupations, such

as law, banking, medicine, education and business. These women need utility, comfort, suitability and that extra dimension that makes you look good. Although a highly successful lawyer, banker, judge or consultant might wish to wear a Chanel or Armani suit on occasion, the rule for working women should be: very smart, but do *not* outdo your client. In general, avoid trendy brands.

You need skirts. You seek them here and you seek them there, always searching for another one that will make your look memorable. Good brand names include Burberry, Aquascutum, Daks, Viyella (if you need to be ultra conservative), Liz Claiborne, Max Mara, Nicole Farhi, Armani Collezione, Margaret Howell, Ann Klein, Joseph, Louise Kennedy and the Gap (for fillers).

As you are always pressed for time, try to book an appointment at some of the top-end boutiques in advance. They will have a selection of your size and preferred styles ready for when you arrive. Trying things on will be so much quicker. Your time is worth too much to waste. Enquire about the tailoring service, and make sure that there is someone around who can pin things for you.

These days a suit is not difficult to find, given the current vogue for retro. Separates also work, but there must be a sense of formality. Try wearing a short navy jacket over a camisole, and add a thin patent or lizard belt at the waist. Wear an Armani-look Nehru jacket in black linen over a taupe pencil skirt with a strand of ivory coloured beads. Buy a navy leather skirt and team it with a thin, cashmere pullover. Pull this look together with a discreet chain belt, and wear a rust-coloured, three-quarter-length coat in herringbone. This looks like a suit, functions like a suit, but is less *boring*. All of these combinations are conservative and appropriate, but not as predictable as pearls and grey flannel.

Bohemian by Nature, Not Necessarily by Occupation

You are different from the rebel, and this has always been your look. You love long, ethnic skirts, crinkled trousers, embroidered waistcoats, Mongolian lamb on everything and long dangly earrings. Your hair is often piled high on your head in a loose messy bun, and you might still be wearing rose-tinted granny glasses and lace-up boots.

Well, we're sorry to say: GET OVER IT! You will look like a bag lady if you continue like this. A little goes a long way. Do one thing, maybe two, but not everything at once. To update the look of long skirts, try Jigsaw, Kenzo, Paul Smith and Rick Owens. Embroidered vests and jackets with beads can be purchased inexpensively at Monsoon, or try Issey Miyake if you like pleated versions. Your jewellery can be ethnic, chunky or antique. Think about Chinese carved cinnabar, ivory, faux tortoise, bakelite and Mexican silver. Do the long, dangly earring thing, but do it with quality. Search through the antique markets for stunning, one-off pieces in jet, cut steel, marcasite and paste. If you are a serious Bohemian, try Christian Lacroix for highly embellished pieces in jewel-like colours. Marni is ultra-chic and quirky, and takes an anti-fashion stance that is very attractive and now. If you are thinking of clashing patterns and colours, a visit to Etro is a must; also check out pieces by Costume National and Missoni. Say goodbye, however, to the torn-and-ripped look – it's not you.

Many of these styles are based on their emphasis on the individual, not the branding. A great Bohemian evening look might consist of black palazzo trousers in silk or wool crepe, a black polo-necked sweater in silk or thin cashmere, a long wraparound velvet jacket with a tied waist – and a silk cord around your neck featuring a hanging Tunisian amulet! Add some pointy black satin boots and you have made your statement.

The Artistic Type: Walking on the Wild Side

You paint or write all day, maybe in your pajamas, torn jeans or tracksuit. You used to smoke. You want others to know that this is who you are when you finally emerge, blinking into the sunlight. It takes a lot of practice to loosen up and put things together for yourself. A lace blouse over jeans is not for everyone, nor are diamonds at breakfast over a grey, Fruit of the Loom T-shirt. Relax and experiment. The secret is in the mixing of old and new, predictable with the unexpected and shaking it up. If you have a wild side, you will have no trouble.

Corporate Ladies, Top of the Food Chain (board members, wives and others)

If this is your life, you work hard and you could be described as a working woman, but your budget is generally a lot bigger. You must dress for success, but not flaunt your husband's wealth or status. Above all, you must not be overtly sexual or predatory in your dress. It is akin to being a doctor: on the one hand, no one wants a doctor who looks like a slob, but nor do we want to see a doctor who wears hand-made crocodile shoes as if he has made a fortune out of your misfortune. This is a delicate line to tread, a time when you have to subdue your instincts to be at the centre of attention and cultivate a stealth approach.

We are talking "serious" clothes, and a lot of them are for evening entertainment. You want admiration, maybe even a touch of envy, but not too much. Now is the time for the stunning little black dress, the beautifully cut Giorgio Armani brown velvet 'smoking' suit, the Chanel jacket (better the real thing) and the little flippy black leather skirt. We suggest you hang out at Jacques Azagury, Laura B, Bruce Oldfield, Amanda Wakeley, Marlowe, Donna Karan, Neil Cunningham and Celine.

A suggestion for the ultra-smart corporate affair: lose the black, go with the brown. Wear a suit (try Akris, Strenesse or Rena Lange) made of bronzy silk shantung, under a taupe cashmere coat with a sable collar and matching Gina high-heeled satin shoes. Accessorize with four strands of pale-green jade beads and finish with a vintage crocodile clutch bag in an envelope shape. If you really want to wow the guests, carry your gloves and flash a Burmese ruby solitaire ring on your smallest finger.

The Naturals

You prefer going *au naturel*, virtually makeup free, braless and couldn't care less. You are often seen in Birkenstocks. Your hair is now going grey – maybe frizzy – if not gone completely and possibly under the control of a large tortoiseshell hair grip. You love Barbours. You wear Puffa jackets and own a world-class collection of them. They all go with your shapeless corduroy trousers that you buy from a catalogue. You have your hands in your pockets and a rather wishy-washy scarf on your head, possibly under a flat cap. Lady, it's time for change!

It is too late for natural unless you are a pig breeder during the day and fall asleep early (or you are *so* beautiful that you need to escape from the non-stop attention you get from men, at any cost). For the rest of us mortals, the natural look past fifty is an impossibility. We might cringe at the thought of Joan Collins's makeup regime and eschew the very thought of plastic surgery to hold up our dewlaps, but if you are truly a sporty type, think what Katherine Hepburn would do. Think Lauren Hutton with deck shoes, jeans, floppy sweaters, a bobbed haircut and attitude. *Au naturel* is just too difficult at this stage of life, because the older you are the more a lack of attention can look like laziness, not devil-may-care insouciance.

Today you do not have to look made up with makeup. There are lots of useful products: tinted moisturizer, Touche Eclat, Estée Lauder's Baume Beauty Éclair, lip gloss, dark brown mascara, nude polish and Armani glossies for the face. Paradoxically, you might find yourself piling on more makeup just to look natural and effortless. You cannot go around pinching your cheeks all day long, so check out the natural-coloured blushes and buy yourself a good brush to apply.

If you insist on being natural underneath, avoid bralessness and go at once to a good bra department and buy yourself a nice, plain, nude, seamless bra with matching knickers. Liberate yourself from your own bigotries. The sporty ladies we know love pretty underwear more than anyone else.

There are plenty of sporty designers and shops: Margaret Howell, Farlow's, Ralph Lauren, Barbour, Holland and Holland, Lilywhites, Sun and Sand and Hermès (get an estimate before you plump for one of their padded jackets or sensible flannel trousers – but they *are* worth it). Your type can wear trainers or loafers from Ralph Lauren and Tod's. Forget the Adidas or Nike unless you are running, or pumping iron or petrol.

There is wonderful antique jewellery to wear with your riding habits, country and outdoor clothes. Victorian brooches feature polo players, enamelled fish, badminton and tennis rackets, racing horses, stags, hunting dogs, portraits of fox heads – you name it, there is great novelty value in these pieces. Some are gold and enamelled, decorated with pearls, diamonds and other gemstones. If you wear one on a lapel, or high on a collar, you will add a touch of chic.

Naturals beware: there is a high cost to being outdoorsy. Hiking in the Rocky Mountains, or playing a round of golf, is often concomitant to ruddy complexions – or worse, mahogany-coloured, weathered and thickened skin. If you play sports, or simply want to look like you do (and you want to retain a sense of youthfulness), you have to deal not only with the shape of your body but the condition of your skin. You must take care of yourself in the sun by wearing a high SPF factor, always, even when it is cloudy.

Rich as Croesus Without a Social Conscience
If you want to risk your life everyday by looking seriously rich, we have a few suggestions. A large car driven by a chauffeur is a must. May we suggest the Hummer in navy blue as the most tasteful, or a Range Rover in anthracite? Haute couture from anyone will do, as well as a very large Graff or Harry Winston diamond for casual wear. Try David Webb animal bracelets and earrings for your Park Avenue pad or Palm Beach villa. For slumming, reserve the entire collection of Chanel well before the season, and call up for a delivery of Beluga and a bottle of Dom Perignon whenever the urge to splurge moves you. You will only need Manolos because you must never walk on the streets. Buy your fur coats (after all, you will either be in the limo or the restaurant) at J. Mendel on Madison Avenue and make it sable. Your nails are sculpted weekly. Someone else can punch in the numbers on your platinum mobile phone.

Rich as Croesus with a Social Conscience
This is more difficult. You have a large BMW X5 driven by a homeless person you have transformed into the working poor. You wear an Armani

navy-blue trouser suit with a Banana Republic T-shirt, a weasel-lined plain grey gabardine raincoat and sport an earnest look. Your rose-cut diamond Georgian jewellery comes from Sandra Cronan in London or Justine Mehlman in Washington DC (just around the corner from government lobbyists) for shimmer, *not* bling. You have classic Art Deco rings and brooches and discreet handmade shoes from John Lobb. Your oldest Birkin is your shopping bag cum attaché case and has tucked into it such socially relevant magazines as *The Green Party Guide* and *The New York Review of Books*. Never go anywhere without a novel by Jorge Luis Borges.

In order to be authoritative at charity meetings, always wear your bifocals. Alternatively, leave your pale-blue contact lenses at home if your eyesight is good enough and bring out the half-reading glasses when making a point. Remove your sunglasses (by Oliver Peoples, expensive but without obvious logos) for direct eye contact with the masses.

In the evening, try a black gabardine trouser suit, impeccably cut, with "farmed", black crocodile shoes. Add a 1920s gemstone Tutti Frutti brooch by Cartier, a tiny diamond watch on a sedate black ribbon (same period and maker) and a seed pearl lorgnette for reading the libretto in your opera box (or the dinner menu at Marks Club). Never wear anything too new and keep everything astronomically expensive.

Ladies Who Lunch and Look Like They Lunch

Find a reliable tailor-designer who understands your body. If you are in London, start your afternoon at London's Berkeley for lunch with a friend and make your way to nearby Jacques Azagury, for a fitting. Over the road, his brother Joseph awaits with a complementary pair of shoes.

You will need a walk after lunch. Venture down to Harvey Nichols department store and hit the makeup department. Buy a new lipstick in the latest shade. There is an oxygen bar on the ground floor that will revive you if you are flagging. If you feel you have put on an extra half-stone at lunch, there is an excellent day spa across the street at the Mandarin Hotel, but if you cannot be bothered, there is Marina Rinaldi of Bond Street and Richmond. Her designs are for heroic women (think Brunhilda) who are still very interested in looking chic and smart. Eskander, Egg, Issey Miyake, Yohji Yamamoto, Laura B and Donna Karan are all good after a meal.

Ladies Who Do Not Lunch, but Look Like Ladies Who Should

These women are always well groomed and stylish in a slobbish world. While everyone else is running around in sweats with trainers, they have found a balance. They are never too done up, or too dressed down. Their instinct for fashion is sharp and they always combine a little of today's trends with the classic elegance they have developed over the years. They do not eat excessively or obsessively; they take vitamins and exercise regularly both for their body shape and overall health. They are "goddesses" and if you spot one, or know one, take a good look at what she is wearing! In art class, you always learn more from the person painting next to you than from the teacher. Style is much the same. Monkey see, monkey do.

The Truth Seekers
There are some women who combine a variety of instincts about fashion but still have their own things to say. They are the chosen few. One day they are ladies, the next they are tramps. They like to play. Their looks for evening can range from Haute Ensemble (e.g., black Chanel chiffon) to High Bohemia. They are natural-born actresses, and their clothes help them play their many roles. They wear navy tailored suits for business meetings with strings of oriental pearls. Later, in the evening, they are seen in black silk leggings, the newest, grooviest beaded caftan and high-heeled satin sandals. They keep their good things and get rid of the dross regularly. They have a supply of past wardrobe solutions (so no need to ever panic) and current fashion finds, which they use with wit and taste. They develop interesting combinations that inspire the onlooker. They have a kind of magic.

How can we acquire this endlessly interesting play on style? Alas, we cannot. These women are always on the lookout, like sniffer dogs, for something imaginative and wonderful. They make incredible connections and choices. The have style in their DNA. We can, however, learn from them. We can be more aesthetically aware, more conscious of ourselves and what suits us, and keep asking questions. And WE CAN LIFT IDEAS AT WILL, just as they do.

CHAPTER ONE

Our Influences and
How We Got Here

ashion is about creativity and self-expression. You can reveal
your character through fashion and how you wear it. From a very
young age women devour magazines, look at each other, and find
a series of experimental looks. This search and its inspirations change
with regularity. Much of fashion is memory, our memories, what we felt
when we were very young: the first thrills, the first kiss, the first high
heels. We remember these experiences selectively as we grow older,
what Diana Vreeland called "rejection," the rejection of what doesn't suit
us, what does not explain us and what does not enhance us. We adjust to
fashion and fashion adjusts to us – at least that is the theory.

Our generation was greatly influenced by the fashions and experiences of our mothers. They, in turn, were affected by enormous, sometimes catastrophic events, such as the Great Depression and two world
wars. Twentieth-century women saw the end of long skirts, the constric-
tions of whalebone corsets and the diminishing significance of hats. The
birth of "utility" clothing brought them greater ease and comfort and the
slow strangulation of class distinctions, which in turn led to the broaden-
ing of the middle classes and the expansion of work opportunities. The
generations of the First and Second World Wars were the pioneers of
women's style.

The New Look
The financial constraints of the Depression introduced at least two
strains in fashion thinking: on the one hand, there was the sparing use of

material with pared-down, clean lines that reflected the difficult universal economic downturn. When the Second World War broke out, shortages in fabric raised skirt lengths, and tailored styles mirrored the military conflict. On the other hand, there emerged an exaggerated glamour on the silver screen, which was highly feminine, sexually charged, body-conscious (just look at those old Jean Harlow satin gowns), escapist and aspirational. These complementary trends have continued throughout the twentieth and into the twenty-first centuries.

In the post-war 1950s period, especially in the United States, where the economy began to improve dramatically, women were bosomy, corseted, wore billowing skirts à la Dior's "New Look," flashed their ankles and donned hats and gloves for all occasions. The New Look boasted yards of material and tiny waists to celebrate the end of hostilities. Men returned from the war, and a woman's place was back in the home, having babies, happily fussing over dinners for children and husbands and opening and closing brand-new refrigerator doors. Her look was ultra-feminine, sexy, but oddly unapproachable as the silhouette depended on very rigid foundation garments. A proper woman changed her clothes several times a day: there were "house dresses" for supervising the housework and greeting the postman at the front door; day dresses and tailored suits for lunch and meetings; tea gowns and cocktail dresses for the cocktail hour; dinner suits for eating in restaurants, and evening gowns for grander occasions. For entertaining at home, women wore long skirts and off-the-shoulder sweaters. Trousers were worn for sporting occasions only, possibly on a cruise. Leisure wear included flared shorts with halters, sun dresses and divided skirts. European-influenced manufacturers copied the French, virtually line for line, and the buying public waited eagerly for newspapers to announce each season's arrival of the new French ideas about lengths and shapes.

Forward-thinking American designers invented "sportswear." Claire McCardell, one of America's most influential designers, then and now, created a relaxed flowing look for women by using native references, such as Navajo patterns, on wraparound blouses worn over long pleated cotton skirts. Simple cotton and ginghams appeared younger and fresher. She combined pleated silk dresses with wide soft leather belts to cinch their waists. Coats were coloured to match and had a playful softness in their lines. She worked with knitwear and made "play" clothes. She loved horizontal stripes, dolman sleeves, halter necks, little neckties, bloomers, and promoted wraps instead of belts. She used hooks and eyes instead of buttons (decades before Dolce & Gabbana). Her colours were odd and off-beat, and she experimented with patchwork and seams.

Every trend we see today can be found in her original conceptions of how women could be fashionable and comfortable at the same time. She invented a way of thinking using sporting references. What Coco Chanel had understood about women in the 1920s, Claire McCardell reengineered in the late 1940s and 1950s. Chanel liberated European upper-class women from their stays, from their cumbersome hats and the weighty layers of the Edwardian era. She made clothes that conveyed personal freedom and enormous chic, emphasizing elegance while thumbing her nose at class differences. She was, after all, the illegitimate child of travelling sales people.

McCardell recognized that American women wanted European sophistication, but they also wanted ease to go with their suburban lives. The suburbs meant cars for everyone. Cars led to shopping developments and country clubs. Cars meant travel, movement, independence and a freedom of the imagination. It was easier to get in and out of a car in something comfortable. Cars meant trousers.

There were other influential designers of the 1950s. One was Bonnie Cashin, who used soft, colourful tweeds combined with leather to produce luscious capes, ponchos, coats and skirts. These leather-bound tweeds were sporty but dripped with sophistication; they were not for country bumpkins. They were clothes for newly affluent people who were on their way somewhere and wanted to look casually smart. Ann Klein and Bill Blass made "ensembles," elegant coats thrown over close-cut sheath dresses and masculine tailored suits. Whether in brocade or flannel, they were formal enough to suit a busy social calendar but relaxed enough to create a new American look. Hannah Troy, Pauline Trigère, Tina Lesser and Norman Norell, among others, designed "dress-up" clothes for grown-up women, whether they were eighteen or eighty. Their outfits created a shape and an attitude for a woman and she didn't need a perfect figure to look good in them.

These designers' ideas were, in their time, revolutionary. They were about a new woman who was beautiful, well educated and ambitious. The easy charm of these clothes was the true genius of American design. Post-war European designers lagged behind, making the same uninspired formal statements, while the frontier spirit of America was creating more liberation for all women. From working in factories, driving Red Cross trucks, taking on all kinds of jobs when their men were overseas, women found new confidence and adaptability, which reflected itself in a deeper questioning of the purpose and role of their clothes.

Our mothers wore these clothes, and we, as fourteen-year-old girls, wanted to look and dress just like them. The rebellious teenager had not yet been invented; she may have existed, but she had not been institutionalized as a class of person. Of course, young women had their own choices laid out with regularity every season. Aside from school uniforms, there were pleated skirts, round-collared shirts, Shetland sweaters, lace-up shoes and loafers. Mothers still worried about their daughters arches. For parties there were taffeta dresses with circle skirts in rich colours, scooped necks, wide elastic belts and baby Louis heels. We collected cashmere sweaters if we could and flat shoes by the dozen. The names Pappagalo and Capezio had the same resonance for us that Prada and Gucci have for this generation of wannabes. We wore camel hair and navy-blue polo coats to football games and three-quarter-length duffel coats to school. "Fast" girls wore tight angora sweaters, tight skirts and big hoop earrings – some things never change.

That was the look until the end of the 1950s. When we went off to university, the rules changed only slightly. The hipper girls played with their wardrobes, made them sexier and cuter, by adding the tightest of sweaters or the sheerest silk blouses to their tweedy suits. We wore kilts and tartan skirts and religiously mimicked the styles shown in *Mademoiselle* and *Glamour*. We could just relate to those terribly pretty, slim girls who looked vaguely like us, though admittedly sleeker.

Winter was warm coats, long knitted mufflers, heavy sweaters and long woolly socks. We wore fur coats, often handed down from grandmother. Trousers were banned from college campuses, and girls wore skirts on the coldest days, just as men wore jackets and ties to class everyday. Dress codes coexisted with the strict moral values of the 1950s. We were afraid of breaking the rules, being punished and developing bad reputations. We were deathly afraid of getting pregnant. We wore thick white cotton pointy bras and snug elastic girdles that guarded our virtue. Our hair was styled in pony tails and "page boys." When we wanted to rebel we borrowed clothes from our boyfriends. (Chanel had always borrowed her lovers' clothes, hacking jackets from Etienne Balsan and tweeds from the Duke of Westminster.) It was cool to wear a hockey-team jacket with varsity lettering on the back, it was cool to have a sweatshirt with your university's name printed on it, in an era that pre-dated the sweat-shirt industry. Cool was a man's shirt with the sleeves rolled up. Cool was always what the guys did.

No one exercised, except for athletes. No one did aerobics, and the gym was a place to be avoided. When forced, we chose golf, folk dancing or volley ball and remained overweight and miserable throughout our college years. In those days the drugs of choice were diet pills, and we took them to stay up all night and study. The healthy option was something your mother talked about, which had far more to do with restraint (not eating pizza and gobbling chocolates and ice cream) than exercise or organic food. We smoked cigarettes not dope, drank gallons of beer and spent a lot of time applying heavy pancake makeup and Maybelline mascara.

When we returned home for school holidays, we wore what our mothers wore. In fact, we freely borrowed their clothes, wore their fur coats to go to the big city, stuffed our feet into towering stiletto heels and pulled up our hair in beehives. We wanted to look like Audrey Hepburn, Kim Novak, Brigitte Bardot, or Sophia Loren. We wore little black dresses for going out on dates, and there was no youth culture…yet.

All this changed in the mid-1960s, perhaps inevitably, after the puritanism of the Fifties and ongoing unresolved social issues. With the arrival of the birth-control pill came the mini-skirt and the Sassoon geometric haircut. Suddenly, everything seemed very different. High fashion magazines we had all read for years changed overnight from featuring frosty models in exquisite gowns and expensive jewellery to the likes of Jean Shrimpton, Twiggy and the oddly featured Penelope Tree, dressed by Mary Quant and Rudi Gernreich. Models were tall and string-slender, almost boneless, childish with huge black-rimmed eyes, dangling their long limbs in the shortest and sparest of skirts. An entire panty-hose industry developed from those skirts. We went from being adolescents to women and then back again to being little girls, complete with micro-skirts, bare knees and thighs, flat-buckled shoes and tiny little sleeveless tops – a look our mothers would have loved on us as nine-year-olds, but at nineteen seemed rather shocking. This was the long awaited Youthquake, a new world made up of people under thirty, of different classes, races and uniformly rebellious against establishment norms. We were in love with the appearance of innocence, artlessness and adventure, sexual and otherwise.

It is ironic that the emphasis on the seemingly adolescent look in fashion that eliminated the legitimacy of adult style coincided with the growing Woman's Movement. Indeed, high-fashion designers have continued to manipulate this contradictory trend. So while women were liberated from the constraints of the past, they were constantly undermined as rational beings. This was a new kind of authoritarianism. Underwear, as we knew it, became outmoded. The Rudi Gernreich "no-bra" became, literally, no bra. The girdle became tights. You could not wear a suspender belt with a mini. Whole concepts of proportion changed radically. Legs needed to be longer and leaner, skirts were short. Chests were flat. Hair was either short, boyish and blunt-cut, or a long waving silky flag. No 'perms' need apply. The fashion industry no longer designed for grown-up women but for those who either looked like or wanted to look like little girls. Just as positions of increased economic, political and social status were opening up, the focus on woman as "adults" in the fashion world mutated into any number of youth-driven directions. Economic and sociological conditions not only raised and lowered skirt lengths, but dramatically separated our values from those of the previous generation. Implicit in this confusion was a more ambiguous sexuality in dress and the casting off of traditional moral constraints. The sexual element of the non-threatening "woman child" (or young boy) became the new turn-on in fashion.

In the 1970s Japanese deconstructionists challenged our fixed ideas about how and why clothes were created. Their ideas were intriguing and seductive, but not designed in a flattering, sexual way. The look often involved complex origami shapes that didn't conform to the body. We were encouraged to wear clothes that were conceived intellectually: trousers with extra legs, sweaters with holes knitted into the design, dresses with shredding seams on the outside, and everything in non-colours, principally black and more black. Along with these clothes we wore strange hats, long ragged scarves and flat-black heavy Doc Martin shoes. By adopting this new radically savvy antifashion, we were declaring ourselves to be on the "cutting edge." The look was seen by many of us as being not only intellectual but antisexist and bohemian. This was hard-edged stuff.

Simultaneously, a few women, such as French designer Sonia Rykiel, were playing with the same girly ideas as Mary Quant had in the early 1960s but with new proportions and better-quality fabrics. She used unstructured knitwear in chopped-off sweater and trouser shapes, a softer alternative to Japanese deconstruction.

Another innovator was Jean Muir, although she must have been influenced by Claire McCardell in her soft approach to shapes. She used a fabulous viscose jersey fabric that clung but did not reveal and suited a dancer's body just as well as a less-than-perfect adult woman's. Her silky skirts swirled gracefully around the body, touching here and there without the slightest trace of vulgarity. Muir encouraged the wearer's personality to emerge through flowing cuts, gather-and-pin tucked bodices, covered buttons and subtle fastenings. The lack of obvious construction and emphasis on three basic colours – navy, black and cream (although she used pale sorbet and other brighter colours expertly throughout her collections) – made her clothes easy to wear. So perfect was their realization that they required little more embellishment than a smile.

In stark contrast, on the other side of the English fashion personality, the punk movement rocked the scene, introducing ripped clothes embellished with a multiplicity of common safety pins, some of them worn through the nose. Ugly was good: aggressive was better. Screaming tartan patterns, chains and sexually explicit zippers were all components of the original Vivienne Westwood–Malcolm McClaren rebellion against the establishment. However much we may have resisted their nasty antics, we have all been affected by their outrageousness. Contemporary designers, such as John Galliano, Versace and Anne Demeulemeester, drew inspiration from these clothes. As time has gone on, Westwood's understanding and love of costume history, coupled with her deep appreciation of art and theatre, have developed into a singular vision that has influenced just about everyone.

In the early 1980s, the financial climate changed from economic stagnation and high interest rates to a burgeoning, no-holds-barred stock market. Suddenly, style took off in a new direction. Along with the market, skirts went up and up, and Karl Lagerfeld at the reinvigorated Chanel was king, where he remains on the top of the pile today. His muse then was the incredibly tall and darkly beautiful Inès de la Fressange, the epitome of Parisian chic. Coco Chanel had always designed elegant, useable clothing and "fantasy" accessories, but Lagerfeld virtually reinvented all the major Coco themes, from tweed jackets, pussy-cat bows and little black dresses, to quilted handbags, fake pearls and leather-and-chain belts. His double 'c's have taken their place among fashion's many clichés, but they remain immensely desirable.

Yves St Laurent was the other influential giant. Establishing his reputation in the early 1960s as the late Christian Dior's successor, he formed his own label, the legendary Rive Gauche. The collection became the first major European prêt-à-porter brand, the new choice for intelligent, fashionable women of our generation. He designed a modern uniform that incorporated a carefully thought-out play on gender roles: trouser suits in gabardine or flannel; loose shift dresses in bittersweet colours; blazers with big brass buttons; exotic harem pants, bellhop jackets, leather jackets and skirts; transparent chiffon evening blouses; and tuxedo jackets with matching trousers for evening wear called "le smoking." He made high-heeled shoes to be worn with trousers, used off-beat, clashing colour combinations, and created flattering knitwear jackets and pullovers. He worked out these themes each season (which were often inspired by theatre and folklore) and drew their cut from the towering standards of couture, adjusting lengths and shapes to the needs of the modern woman. His muses were Loulou de La Falaise and Betty Catroux, tall, rangy girls with unconventional faces who made everything they wore look fabulous.

Rive Gauche collections gave women everywhere the opportunity to be an exotic Russian princess one moment and an odalisque the next. With St Laurent you had a gifted collaborator in the redefinition of yourself, every season. His playfulness, always underlying a precise cut, enabled his clients to be who they wanted to be. Housewives wore his clothes. Catherine Deneuve would accept no other. He gave women real choices and supplied the basics to mix and match for an individual look that was never vulgar or coarse. No matter how old or young you were, his disciplined genius made you feel womanly but always a bit sexy and off-centre. St Laurent was expensive but a fraction of the cost of couture with all of the look. If he were designing today, we would all be happier.

There were other stars in the 1980s, especially the ultrafeminine Ungaro. His clothes were what the French call "*flou*": they had softness and movement, colour and pattern, and they were often tucked, ruched and very flirty. Even working in black leather, Ungaro managed to gather, mould and ease the material onto the body. His man-tailored checked trouser-suits were cut close, nipped in and utterly feminine, especially when worn with a florid printed blouse. There was nothing to compare to the sexy Ungaro cocktail dress in jersey or silk print. They had their own inimitable signature.

The zeitgeist changed in the 1990s, however, as the social and economic landscape again altered, bringing total fashion confusion: from Grunge to minimalism. Stemming from the financial distress of the early decade, Grunge was a social reaction against the padded shoulders and conspicuous consumption of the 1980s' excesses, elitism and collapsed dreams, against the lust for success, materialism and snobbery. In fashion terms, Grunge was dirty-looking, drug-addled and angry. It spawned a devil-may-care, up-yours attitude whose arrogance haunts young designers today. (All grown-up, Marc Jacobs is still struggling with his early love affair with Grunge.) Although it claimed to be disinterested in fashion, Grunge was a highly self-conscious style that screamed ironic indifference while playing on our materialistic desires. It satisfied no need other than to shock. Every tattooed exposed hip, every lip stud, every greasy lock of hair hanging over a grimy looking T-shirt is a reminder that, at least amongst the younger set, Grunge is alive and well.

At the other end of the style spectrum, minimalism could also be seen as a reaction to the power dressing of the 1980s, but it works its attitudes out in a very different way. In a sense, stripping away excess became the last refuge of the thinking woman in a confusing terrain. Designers explored a modern idiom that relied on perfect cut and execution, neutral colours and sophisticated simplicity. The attractions of this pared-down aesthetic were based on new ideas and techniques about the draping and cutting of fabric. A dress was a piece of architecture that required, even dictated, very little embellishment by the wearer. Its language was clean. The sexuality of the wearer was implicit, not overt. Courrèges, Giorgio Armani, Jil Sander, Calvin Klein and Narciso Rodriguez, to mention a few, expressed this sensibility best. The trouble was, however, that unless you were very beautiful or striking, minimalism could become boring, repetitive, formless and unfeminine. If not perfectly made, the clothes looked cheap.

Not surprisingly, the fashion community has been teetering back and forth between these two poles since the middle of the 1990s: from the tattiness of Grunge to the sterility of minimal, from vulgar to dull.

As fashion evolves there have always been revolutions in taste. Since the 1980s women have been subjected to a new and disturbing phenomenon: Fashion as Big Business, dominated by accountants, not designers. Bernard Arnault, of the luxury brands conglomerate LVMH (Louis Vuitton/Moet Hennessy), has been hailed as the saviour of fashion houses and designers. The industry has always been characterized by boom-and-bust financing. A manufacturer who suffers one or two bad seasons can easily go bankrupt, and young designers today have a terrible time staying ahead of the bailiffs. In a high-wire business world of ideas, ephemera, ego and change, LVMH has attempted to reduce the financial risks of one designer by spreading the risk among others who were more commercially established or successful in a given season.

The reality, however, seems somewhat different. In a large corporation, everyone is eventually measured by the same quarterly profits criteria, and there is little tolerance for unprofitable divisions, a fact we are made aware of every day in *The Wall Street Journal* or *Financial Times*. The engine of LVMH is, of course, Louis Vuitton. The result for the buying public seems to have been homogenization, stifled creativity and an increased emphasis on the things that continue to sell well: accessories – bags, shoes and perfume. There simply isn't enough commercial time for a new designer to develop a signature, to evolve in an incremental way. Indeed, an established fashion house can easily get caught in the trap of predictability, and in recent years we have witnessed an increasing emphasis on sensation, eccentricity and change for change's sake, all in order to capture the attention of the powerful fashion press and to make big bucks (or Euros) in a mass market. Thus, advertising and the most sensationalized promotion are even more important than the product. Remember Gucci's Rush perfume advertising campaign? Two heroin addled teenagers passionately touch each other intimately to sell a pair of plain black trousers and some scent. Here we see one legacy of the Grunge movement: what began as a protest against commercialism has become a very commercial movement indeed – the selling of non-fashion through down-and-dirty imagery. This overreliance on sex to sell everything has created an expanding market of jaded, anaesthetized consumers.

In this new business climate, Gucci, under Tom Ford, became the ultimate destination brand, the go-to place for cachet. In its dominating progression, focussed on perfume, accessories and daring advertising, Gucci's aura became more and more aggressive. The actual product line, however, remained essentially what it had been from the very first Ford collection: a new twist on a lot of black classics, low-slung, bottom- and crotch-hugging trousers, snug long jackets (probably to hide those bulging derrières) and trashy-looking dresses. The bags remained well made with an oddly mass-market appeal, at very high prices. Shops were jam-packed. The brand became both a lifestyle and a cliché. Tom Ford became famous, the darling of the press, and his personality cult became intimately associated with all aspects of the Gucci brand. He has moved on, but the industry is still relying on celebrity branding.

The takeover of YSL by Gucci seemed the pinnacle of hubristic presumptuousness. Reliable, every-season-buy-something customers were lost to other designers. Gucci's attempt to impose sex and rock 'n' roll onto YSL has not yet been a commercial success. Its old values have been lost, and the personal vision of Yves St Laurent has evaporated, leaving in its place an array of slashed, shredded and revealing frocks. The very young, who might be attracted to the look, cannot afford it, and the more mature woman cannot wear it. Like so many fashion houses, YSL runs the risk of being a label dependent on hype and the thoughtless recycling of old ideas. That is not enough to win back core customers and their daughters who knew better times. Even their horn-handled handbags do not overly tempt.

Versace, Dolce & Gabbana and John Galliano at Dior have also employed the sex-sells-everything approach to fashion. Although their sales tactics may be similar, their underlying design philosophies are different. Gianni Versace became the avatar for baroque, expensive, flashy sleaze in the 1990s. His fantastic homes, propensity for chain-mail, Medusa heads, peek-a-boo effects and bare flesh, dutifully praised by the press, made him fashion's equivalent of *Hustler*'s Larry Flynt. Models clamoured to wear Versace's tight, short frocks in acid colours. Despite their overt sexuality on the catwalk, the dresses were not as shocking as the erotically charged advertising behind them, but the buying public responded readily to this provocative, orgiastic imagery. After his untimely murder, his sister Donatella took over the label and enlisted the aid of his many model and actress friends (including Madonna) to assist in its continued promotion as sexy dressing. Donatella's frocks continue to be a Neapolitan take on the cocktail hour and really present no challenge. If they appeal to you, it's a question of getting past the hype and the rather louche sales staff.

If Versace's image is serious Mediterranean glitz and a paean to zips, studs, holes, slits to the thigh, see-through fabrics and hoisted bosoms, then Dolce & Gabbana has a more humorous, tongue-in-cheek take on the same theme. Taking their cue from Jean Paul Gaultier in the 1980s, whose original, cone-shaped bras for Madonna set the look, D&G believe in underwear, often as outwear. Every garment has an under-slip or built-in brassière intended to cantilever breasts and build confidence. Dresses have endless grommets, with fabrics often shirred like Austrian blinds to hug the body. In this world of make-believe Sicilian widows and streetwalkers, there are leopard linings inside jackets and feline details on sweaters and dresses. If there were a style that shouted "Gina Lollobrigida" or "Anna Magnani," this is it. And yet, a closer look reveals razor-tailored coats, sharp black and pinstripe suits and witty clothes with feminine attitude. But although fashion addicts are prepared to sacrifice comfort and ease for a look, for most people there are just too many bondage closures that do nothing.

Mining the same vein is today's Rasputin of sexy dressing, Roberto Cavalli, who specializes in loading everything on top of everything: prints, furs, furbelows, laces, holes, straps and diamante, all pulling in different directions at the same time. His magpie designs attract women who believe they benefit from this in-your-face look, but the clothes demand a perfect body and an innocent face. Anyone else risks looking like an old tart.

The quintessential designer of "Excess sells Everything" is John Galliano. Like so many very creative people, he began his career with an inventive, colour-drenched, historical view of fashion design, aided by a skillful cut and eye for flattering shapes. Like many young designers, his finances went from boom to bust every other season, but it was just a matter of time before he would be discovered by Big Business. Bernard Arnault had the vision to appoint him head of Dior. Under the umbrella of LVMH, he has become the master marketer for Dior, and his design leadership and self-promotional skills have brought record profits to its accessories business. The outrageous attitude of his designs has produced incredibly theatrical couture collections – his shows have featured tramps and trapeze artists, duchesses and demi-mondaines – that have garnered ecstatic notices from the press. They are enthralled by his seemingly limitless imagination and the use he has made of his classically skilled atelier. For us, he is the Marcel Duchamp of the frock. His designs may be scandalous, amusing and brilliant, laden with fashion references and gimmicks, but ultimately they are unwearable, and his commercialism is beginning to pall.

In contrast to the "bad boys" of fashion, Miuccia Prada has consistently designed against the sex-sells trend. Her approach to style and its expression in retailing has produced absolutely essential pieces every season. Why are her ironic, post-modern clothes such a phenomenon? Perhaps because they are part of our psyche, part of our collective memories, which have different emotional meanings for all of us, young and old.

Her career as a fashion guru began at her grandfather's exclusive, Milan-based handbag and luggage business. From these roots, she and her husband built a fashion empire whose foundations were practical black nylon handbags for women with careers. In her own idiosyncratic way, she has worked through most of the trends and ideas of the twentieth century. If there has been a notable cut or style in the last fifty years, Prada has taken it, given it a good kick up the backside and transformed its proportions into something entirely new and strangely desirable. She has turned humble kitchen-cloth patterns into dresses, promoted lowered waists and chopped off clam-digger trousers for winter wear. She has made utility clothes chic and bejewelled the most basic sweaters and raincoats. Her iconic pinched-toed, high-heeled shoes have influenced every shoe manufacturer; despite being highly uncomfortable they have a compelling stylishness. If women worry about wrinkles in their clothes, she designs clothes that are meant to be wrinkled. If uneven seams are a bugbear, her skirts feature asymmetrical seams. She can even make a crocheted dress, knitted like a tea cosy, look drop-dead chic. Zippers are concealed up the sides as they were in the 1950s, to keep the beauty of the back of the garment. She uses strings and ribbons in the place of buttons and belts. She has single-handedly brought back the crafts of appliqué, crochet and beading on the most pedestrian materials. She has invented new fabrics, and batiked and tie-dyed everything.

The perfect candidate for a Prada suit or dress is a small, well-proportioned woman of any age, because the pieces are cut close to the body. But larger ladies love her clingy sweaters, swingy skirts and fur-edged coats. Prada makes wispy transparent blouses that can utterly transform conservative business suits. In the context of the youth cult (and despite her primary market, the young, the slight and the skinny), season after season she produces collections that continue to surprise and inspire her ever-increasing customer base. It is as if she has been summoned by the Zen Master of All Fashion to correct other people's work with her own unmistakably edgy handwriting. Those who adore her philosophy but cannot get their left haunch into a Prada skirt buy the bags and shoes and gaze wistfully at the racks of clothes. Like too many designers of today, Prada has adhered to a strict set of sizes, European 38 to 44, which simply does not reflect the real world of women. Women are getting taller and broader everywhere on the planet.

It is important to mention Ralph Lauren. He is a driven entrepreneurial prince whose lifestyle vision is epitomized by the sumptuousness of his stores, where the customer can find unchallenging clothes and accessories in a comfortable seductive setting. He initially captured the attention of women in the 1970s with sharp menswear that was sexy, young, always in good taste and easy to wear, and he has drawn inspiration from the American West, with its Native Americans and pioneers, as well as country squires and Hollywood stars of the 1930s. His fashion heroes are Lauren Bacall and Gary Cooper. The mise en scènes have changed over the years – from English country house to Manhatten penthouse, from Western prairie adobe to Acapulco villa – and his styles today continue to be derivative of the current zeitgeist. There is always a bit of adjustment to what is at the cutting edge, but never too much. His clothes suit every occasion, every location and, if you are going on holiday, whether north, south, east or west, he can supply a costume for the event in one of his vast, dry-goods emporiums.

Every season superb advertising campaigns conjure up beautiful people wearing conservative tweeds and velvets that incorporate a new trend. One season there are bunched-up suede trousers that only those with serious vitamin deficiencies would attempt to wear; other year's dresses, blouses and neat little suits will take you effortlessly from town to country and back. There is the seriously expensive Miss Marple look, and at the other end of the spectrum, the nearly naked, very demanding evening-gown collection, satin or beaded, cut on the bias and requiring corporeal perfection. Lauren and his design team are hooked on vintage-style fabrics, which is right in line with retro thinking. His clothes are safe, never ridiculous (and would never frighten the horses), but never exactly fashionable. His profits derive from coloured shirts with polo logos and sports clothes of all descriptions. Ralph Lauren is an American success story, the embodiment of the American Dream. He is still a driven and genius merchandiser with a taste and imagination fuelled by cinematic memories of his youth.

And then there is Mr. Giorgio Armani. Armani stands for ease and comfort, about throwing off formality and structure, about replacing padding with easy draping. His clothes are about gender playfulness, aimed neither at the young nor the old, neither the beautiful nor the plain. In the Armani woman, there is a knowingness, a secret charm, something always held in reserve. The understatement of an Armani outfit imposes a special ethos on the woman who wears it. She is a sphinx (or so the advertisements once told us). Armani today, as yesterday, has a recognizable look and attitude, at best utility and elegance, at worst, dull. He still makes fashion that murmurs and doesn't shout, and has drifted away from his roots of dressing Milanese women with lots of money, jewellery and tans. His central tenet that clothes are a uniform, much like menswear, and should complement, not dominate, a woman, continues to work. For those with careers and other serious concerns, Armani clothing is ideal for the office, the boardroom and travel. His clothes have a subtle pleasure that does not overly excite, but their high quality and finish impart confidence on any occasion. You cannot but be taken seriously in your well-cut "greige" trouser suit and silk blouse; you can wear a black Armani silk trouser suit to the Opera or to a black tie dinner. You can be model slim or imperfect in shape, you can be feeling fragile, but his polished look transcends physical limitations and makes you feel protected. Armani is therapeutic and good for you, like herbal tea.

As the generation of designers who have influenced our world in the late twentieth and early twenty-first century begin to age, the future of fashion for us seems uncertain. Who are the new names and faces to take their place? Who will understand what we have seen and done, where we have been, emotionally and sartorially? *We* have cultivated our tastes along the way, and to stay relevant we must continue to expand our awareness of style. Each decade requires a reassessment. *We* need to identify new designers and thinkers who ponder the age-old question of "What to wear". The following are some who might lead the way to *our* fashion future.

New designers take getting used to. Their pieces must to be tried on to understand what they are about. If you pass them on a hanger, they might look a bit odd. Remember how strange Issey Miyake first appeared in the 1970s? Today you might very well find an eighty-year-old women and her somewhat decrepit husband in the shops, trying on those oddly cut and proportioned asymmetric skirts and shirts, which have a timeless, ageless quality that can be edgy and feminine at the same time.

Etro is an Italian manufacturer of the rich hippy look, full of jewel-like colours and paisley patterns, in styles highly embellished with braid, gilt, ruffles and a riot of pattern and texture. Their classics include printed challis skirts to wear with vaguely Tyrolean jackets, velvet coats and blouses to team with striped flannel skirts or trousers. They feature shot taffeta and fitted jersey pullovers. The rich hippy might appear every few years, but Etro got there first and does it best. One large Etro scarf – beaded, tasselled and decorated with sprinkles of gold sequins – will give real pizzazz to a plain tailored suit. Draped around the hips of a simple black skirt, voilà, you have a bit of gypsy in your soul.

Marni makes eccentric versions of everyday items. A skirt tailored from ordinary menswear fabric might have a silk petticoat peeking out at the hem. Put it with a plain classic sweater and high boots and you are instantly hip and today. Cashmere cardigans would look a bit like Grandpa's except for the unusual colour combinations and extra-snug fit. Picture yourself in one of Marni's bright-neon wool ottoman kimono jackets with grey flannel trousers and matching polo-neck sweater. Add a fake felt flower to the shoulder, and you can make a very personal statement. Marni contrasts plain items with funky, imaginative handbags and shoes. In measured doses, this can be liberating and fun. It's worth remembering that modern dress is an exercise in combining, and you must ask the salesperson how they recommend a piece be worn.

Bottega Veneta represents the new marketing methodology. The first collections have taken beautiful, no-logoed woven bags into new colours and a higher price range, but its line of clothes is also worth watching: double sweater coats, swingy taffeta skirts with low (but not too low) slung waists, terrific Donegal tweed jackets, and suede and leather in wonderful colourways – almond, acid green, pink, sky-blue and citrus-yellow. Collections have included softly draped dresses to be worn over bare skin and transparent T-shirts with matching cardigans. They have the easy language of modern clothes. It is important to note that virtually the entire collection is sold from trunk shows (see page 126).

Of the avant-garde Antwerp Six, which put Belgium on the fashion map in the late 1990s, Dries Van Noten and Ann Demeulemeester are worth pointing out. Van Noten specializes in gorgeous wrap coats in highly decorated fabrics, embroidered full skirts and a sophisticated peasant look. Demeulemeester loves straps, buckles, leather, soft thick cotton, monotones and innovative materials. It is not necessary to wear the whole look. One piece, a sequinned waistcoat, for example, with black trousers or a long skirt with black stockings and boots, is modern enough. Do remember, however, that all of these manufacturers have a young, hip clientele in mind. We must learn how to combine these daring pieces to look up to date but not ridiculous.

Recently, there has not been any one towering figure on the Paris scene to ignite universal interest, but at the reinvigorated Lanvin, Alber Elbaz has been allowed to let his skills and imagination soar to applauded heights. His current interest is in the classical with a twist. Marc Jacobs is in the press every day, either for Louis Vuitton or his eponymous brand. He makes very hip clothes for very hip girls, retro pastel suits and pretty dresses in very small sizes. Sooner or later, he is going to have to catch up with the rest of us; after all, he is getting older and so is his clientele. It may not be long before he's dealing with the demands of the smart fifty-ish female film producer, not just her daughter. Rick Owens makes unstructured jackets, cardigans and long, layered knitted skirts that suit the young and not so young. His interesting ribbon-and-tie closures, asymmetrical cut, paper-thin leather jackets and flowing lines make an artistic statement that is not exactly fashion, but timeless and flattering, as long as you can figure out how to get them on and off.

Caroline Charles, Louise Kennedy, Paddy Campbell, Akris and Marlowe design for "women." They know what is needed in the real world and have a feel for quality and wearability. They occasionally make individual pieces that even the trendiest soul might yearn for: a chunky white lace jacket perfect with baggy linen trousers, washed-out jeans or "peasant" skirt. Paddy Campbell makes beautiful printed-silk and lace dresses that look equally good with flip flops or high-heeled sandals, ideal in a country garden or the South of France. Louise Kennedy goes for scrumptious candy-coloured tweeds, which she cuts into wonder suits with either pencil or mini-skirts edged in fringe or contrasting grosgrain ribbon. Her long cashmere coats are to die for. These designers specialize in what we would call "correct" or "occasion" clothes, but separate pieces can be dressed down with jeans or cargo pants for a casual look. Underrated American designer (like Birger and Christensen of Night and Day) Megan Park works in a decorative and feminine idiom to produce charming soft, beaded handbags, beautifully embroidered, silk wrap-around blouses and v-neck printed dresses that skim the body. They always feature contrasting cardigans, and the prices are right.

It is always worth seeking out again such standard names as Jaeger, Betty Jackson, DKNY, Nicole Farhi, Phase 8, Liz Claiborne, Anne Klein, Zara and Wallis. The demands of today's fashion business require constant rethinking, and you just might hook into the current trend at a reasonable price. But remember, get in there early in the season.

CHAPTER TWO

So Here We Are Still
Looking for a Look...
Inspirations ...
How do we Stay Relevant?

We all have style heroines in our collective mind and heart. Time and time again, Audrey Hepburn is dragged out of the 1950s and plastered across magazines because there are no real icons worth emulating today. The same is not quite so true with Grace Kelly, but no doubt it will come. Both stars, great beauties, worked the same side of the street: they were sleek, aristocratic and quietly alluring. Audrey Hepburn was a born clothes horse, but she also had the help of a genius, Hubert de Givenchy, who not only designed all of her clothes on and off screen, but created a perfume for her too, L'Interdit, so taken was he with her elfin charm. Grace Kelly might have appeared to be the quintessential American princess, but she was in fact the daughter of an Irish bricklayer who became a millionaire. She went to Hollywood, made films and had love affairs with the great actors of the day, eventually winning a real prince. Leaving Hollywood behind, she adopted an impeccable royal style: pastels, pale furs, small neat hats, discreet jewels, ivory-coloured gloves and conservative hair and makeup.

Both actresses represented polished perfection and poise, which today can bring on the indictment of "elitism." We are a little afraid to look too neat, too well groomed and too smart. It does not go with street credibility and the endless vogue for dressing down. And that look can be, on a middle-aged woman, very ageing. When we idolized these creatures they were in their twenties and thirties, and so were we. But their high standards of presentation are still inspirational, if only for special events.

We have also loved Marilyn Monroe and Julie Christie for the innocence of their sexuality; Diane Keaton and Barbra Streisand for their quirky individuality; and Jane Fonda and Margaret Thatcher for their potency and power.

They say that sixty is the new fifty. Well, maybe seventy is the new forty! Who knows, it depends on the individual and how many drugs she is taking. We are well preserved, toned, dieted, dyed and lifted. We have worn everything and seen fashions come and go. We want to look like ourselves but with a modern twist. How can we achieve this when so many of today's designers and manufacturers make clothes only appropriate for teenage girls? Or if they are suitable for us, they come at a premium price. Unless you plan your wardrobe like a battle campaign and get to the shops as new clothes hit the racks, usually at the height of the previous season, it becomes impossible to find anything at all. After the opening round, you must be prepared to forage every day for ideas and opportunities, as your size is usually long gone and the remaining choices are unappealing. No one can make a full-time career out of getting dressed.

Although there are thousands of handbags and shoes out there, there is little new and inspiring to wear with them. Women with desire and money are being left in a kind of shopper's no-woman's land. Some women make do with the games mistress or barmaid look, or just resign themselves to what is in the deep recesses of their wardrobes. They drag out the same old thing every time they have to go out and feel frumpy and boring. This is not an acceptable state of affairs.

The problem in Anglo-Saxon society is that there is no social expectation for women to stay feminine and sensual past a certain age. They are not taught, from birth, the care regimes of European and Latin women. They are overloaded by the cultural norm of Barbie and preternaturally buxom cartoon characters. There are millions of us with money in our purses, but there is no style template on which our imagination can light. Do we emulate television personalities, with their plastic faces and their pastel trouser suits? Movie Stars? Pamela Anderson? Politicians, whose dress sense seems calculated to least offend the greatest number? The fashion crowd, who are always in black, no matter what, and tote the latest handbag as their biggest fashion statement? What do we do?

Latins Unlimited
For real inspiration, let us start with a culture of people whose style we admire, the Latins: Italian, French and South American women. Though more tradition bound in many ways, these societies don't discard the older woman, deny her opportunities for pleasure or dismiss her as a physical being. There are any number of Italian and French women of a

certain age who are as erotically charged as they ever were without being overdressed, too made-up, overlifted or ignored. There is no guilt in the Latin woman's attitude about making herself look good. They are taught style at an early age by their mothers, and their innate self-confidence enables them to develop their fashion personalities over time, without a sense of panic about the natural ageing process. They have been taught to be proud of their femininity and that is why they remain looking good. As Nina Ricci once said, "Know yourself before you get dressed." They value experience, knowledge, sophistication and their sexuality (think Simone Signoret and Jeanne Moreau).

As a result, the Latins deal with the limits of age better than Anglo-Saxons. In a world that assaults the idea of the "eternal feminine," we must learn these same survival skills. We must have constructive self-criticism, not self-hatred. Learning to judge yourself objectively within your own peer group is vital, not to compare yourself to a twenty- or thirty-year-old woman. Carl Jung, the great psychoanalyst of dreams, once wrote, "We cannot live the afternoon of life according to the program of life's morning, for what was great in the morning will be little at evening, and what in the morning was true will at evening have become a lie."

Forget the Mags

Vogue, which was once a useful, readable document, full of ideas and stylish combinations, is now more of a teen magazine. The concentration is on the body, not its coverings. This may reflect the paucity of genuine design imagination in the fashion industry, or the competition to sell advertising space. Models are beautiful and very young, pliable and extraordinary in their photogeneity, but they are impossible to relate to. We used to gape in adoring recognition at the likes of Jean Patchett or Suzy Kendall, Jean Shrimpton or Lauren Hutton. We were younger then and though we admired them and the clothes they wore, we could still imagine ourselves as them. Perhaps they were inspirational because they represented a more perfect version of ourselves. But near-naked photos of Kate Moss and Naomi Campbell (themselves now into their thirties) hardly make us want to rush out and buy what they are wearing.

The medium, as Marshall McCluhan wrote in the 1960s and we all now know, is the message, the emperor's new clothes. So you can forget the glossy magazines for guidance through the minefield of fashion. They can be scanned for the ads, read for information on breast cancer, book and movie reviews and for endless advice on plastic surgery. You can catch up with Hollywood's latest starlet discovery and sexually titillating gossip, but forget the joys of fashion.

CHAPTER THREE

Starting Over (Again)

Before you can start searching for and building a wearable and affirmative wardrobe, we must begin with the Big Clean Out. This is a good idea because it will reveal the full extent of your self-delusion (clothes-wise at least) and will pinpoint the necessity to think anew. Let us call this "the Decade Dump." But, you might ask, how do you clear out your wardrobe's emotional wreckage of useless items accumulated over years?

We are older, we have lived. Some of the favourites you treasure and horde no longer suit the person you have become. Would you wear at twenty what you thought fabulous at fourteen? Women age in decades. So, go into the cupboard and observe closely the following advice.

Do you wear it regularly? Is it something for a special event? Do you love it and feel great every time you wear it? Do you take it out, put it on and immediately discard it for something else? Do you have a group of favourites that work well together? Does your partner look at you quizzically when you parade yourself before him in this item? Does he say sweetly, "Is that what you are wearing tonight, dear?" Do you feel fat in it? If you do you will never again wear it, even if you lose pounds. The last time you walked into a room, did you wish you had worn something else? In other words, is it taking up space and not pulling its weight? If so, turf it out. Be ruthless. We all have the habit of taking something out of the closet and putting it right back.

We don't believe in the two-year rule for discarding, but the Emotional Intelligence rule: how do you feel when you put on this piece of

36

clothing – good, great, sexy, smart, yourself? If none of these, get rid of it. It was probably a mistake in the first place, and, if you are honest, you will admit that you never much liked it and only wore it out of the guilty feeling that it cost too much to throw away.

Save anything that has a specific use if it still fits, like jodhpurs, a long woolly skirt (for winter weekends in the country), tweed jackets to wear with jeans, coats that still look good as long as the shoulders are narrow and the fabric isn't damaged or stained. Save anything made of brocade or fur. Save strange eccentric things. Throw out anything boring, which will not get more interesting with age. Throw out shoes that have damaged heels, crushed or misshapen toes, are too high, too low and that are no longer stylish. Keep a few pairs for the rain, but that's all. Throw out boots that have nothing more than sentimental value (you bought them twenty years ago on a trip to Florence). Give away, to your best friend's daughters (if yours won't have them), something wonderful that you could still wear, was suitable years ago, but doesn't give you a lift now. Give away colours that drain you. Give away things that are too big, too small, too long and too short. Do not bother spending money on expensive alterations; never attempt to fix shoulders. If you have five trouser suits in the same style, keep the one you really love and sell the rest. Just bite the bullet and take everything to the Red Cross, Cancer Research, Oxfam or a good second-hand shop.

Go through your sweater drawers and give away anything that has pulls, pills and has been washed and dry-cleaned dozens of times and doesn't shout WEAR ME anymore. Save classics like bright cable-knit cashmeres, which can be used on holiday to tie around your neck or waist. Save twin sets in pretty colours. They work with jeans and silky skirts. Arrange your sweaters according to the seasons. If, like some women, you start wearing navy in March/April, take your heavy brown and black sweaters and either put them away in an upper shelf or in a suitcase under the bed. Be sure to add a cedar chip or moth balls to keep away the nibblers.

Evening clothes have a life-span, although most of us don't like to acknowledge this. There are ball gowns for special occasions that could be worn again, especially if they come in two parts, bottom and top. They can be divided up and worn differently, perhaps with a contrasting cashmere or silk sweater for a more casual look. If they were made for a specific event, however, you probably won't get much more use out of them – excluding, of course, those of you who attend hunt balls regularly. If the dress was made by a couturier, keep it as a treasured memory that can be passed on to your daughters one day, or you might contact the local costume museum. Anything else should be judged by the same implacable standard: does this make me feel good? Black cocktail dresses can be hoarded as long as they are kept in good condition. There is nothing worse than opening the cupboard to take out an old favourite and finding white marks and greasy thumbprints, just as you were meaning to wear it again. Part of keeping things is maintenance. If it is all too much and you just need one uniform, discard the old ones and make space for the new.

Clear out your underwear drawer and get rid of bras that do not fit, ragged knickers with holes and heavy pantyhose in odd colours that you haven't worn for years. Save old lace handkerchiefs, silk camisoles and the odd garter belt for those rare stocking moments. Save socks for wearing under boots. Discard old nightgowns that have lost their bows or pearl trim, and give away stained bathrobes, especially those made of towelling with hanging threads. If you are still saving parts of your trousseau, put everything in a clean box in tissue and leave for future generations, but get them out of this life.

Now that you have cleared the decks, let's talk about what we can wear with pleasure.

BASIC
INSTINCTS

CHAPTER FOUR

Black Beauty and Colour Me

You probably bought your first black dress when you were fourteen. It went with the black crayon you used, to create existentialist eyes, à la Juliet Greco or Twiggy. Black was a reaction to pleated skirts, scratchy Shetland sweaters, gym slips, knee socks and lace-up shoes. It was reminiscent of forbidden books, such as Jack Kerouac's Beat classic *On the Road*. Black stood for rebellion. Black was Marlon Brando. Black was Peggy Lee. Black was Miles Davis, jazz and the night. It was all about the individual against the Establishment.

Think about it: since what year was black no longer a rebellion for you? For the last thirty years, black has been the colour of safety. It seems always correct (except at a rodeo) and never lets you down. Though it can be draining in the day, it has its uses.

It is the building block of any woman's wardrobe, as long as she knows how to wear it. Chanel was the first to see its sexy potential. Her little black dresses were called "poverty deluxe" by the sneering fashionistas of the day. But they got it wrong. Black goes on and on. Since the 1920s, the fashion press regularly announces its demise, but it is never true.

As a powerful societal statement, black started in the 1970s, with a number of sociological phenomena, such as Feminism, Woman's Liberation and Political Correctness. Black is post-Holocaust, post 9/11. Black is social guilt. Black is gender free. When we wear black, we indicate on a subliminal level that we understand the deep issues of life. When we wear black, we may be sending out a number of messages, or saying absolutely *none* at all, because black lends itself to the imagination of the onlooker. Black can represent a safe pair of hands, the kind of basic fashion value system that eliminates differences of race, colour, creed, sex and status. Black can be like cooking. We all cook with the same ingredients. It is what you do with them that make a dish great or bland, chopped liver or paté de foie gras. For the artist in us, all black is a blank canvas, like white. Accessories and attitude are the brushstrokes that make it special to you. Black is chic at night because its darkness is always more mysterious and glamorous than colour.

Let us talk about the ubiquitous black suit, with trousers or a skirt. You are going to the ballet, opera, or theatre with dinner after. You are sitting for a solid three hours in a small space, cramped and pressed on either side by a warm breathing body. The air-conditioner is on full blast. Parts of you, like your feet and legs, are freezing. Your upper body and lungs are stifling. What to wear? Naturally, when you get up for a stroll around the bar you don't want to look sweaty and flushed. Because you are smart, you wear an Armani-look black trouser suit. It is comfortable, in a lightweight wool crepe and hasn't crumpled. You may be coming from work, so you took a lace camisole to the office in your big black nylon handbag, ditched your white T-shirt and, like a magician, pulled out a pretty citrine crystal necklace and a black satin clutch. You tossed a dark grey and gold cashmere scarf over your shoulders and, presto! You are transformed.

With black, the choice of jewellery is vital. If you own beautiful pearls, try wearing them with your jeans instead. A more eccentric choice makes your black outfit younger and cooler. If you are wearing a skirted suit, you will need to change from sensible shoes or boots to something more elegant. Wear very sheer black or nude tights (Falke is tops) and either strappy black or bright-coloured satin sandals or slingbacks to dress you up and emphasize your legs. Remember the lengthening effect of the beige shoe. Chanel has always done them with little black satin toes that impart immediate stylishness.

We love the little black dress, but what are the best options for us? We don't want something so formal, so severe that it makes extra demands on us. We want ease, elegance and something that is not too rigid or too clingy. At the same time, we must avoid the overdesigned numbers that are everywhere, those with too many bells and whistles. There is far too much "bad taste is good taste" design around these days. For the trimmer woman, Prada does a line of classic black dresses every season, always with a bit of tied or draped chiffon or bobble and braid ornament to make them unique and modern. Donna Karan is famous for black jersey dresses that compliment a fuller body. Micheal Kors cuts a stretchy little black gabardine dress in simple American taste. Issey Miyake always carries a version of the black dress with some funky connotations; his knitted silk ones virtually roll up in a ball and are indestructible. Use your accessories to charm. Instead of a necklace, try a big climbing green enamel lizard brooch, or pin on a giant flamingo on your shoulder rather than wearing the old regimental diamonds. Take time to look through the antique markets for vintage costume jewellery. Big fake diamonds can be almost as much fun as real, if not more. They are certainly safer to wear.

A black lace dress will take you everywhere, except a football game. Never ever give one away unless it is in shreds. They are timeless. Louise Kennedy and Jacques Azagury always have one or two in their collections. Forget black velvet dresses for the most part as they are always too heavy (remember your hot flushes). A better choice is a black velvet Chinese jacket with a bright silk lining over black trousers and a jersey pullover. Wear a black kimono over a crush-pleated long skirt and a black crocodile belt.

Black beaded dresses are a puzzlement. They are so lovely to look at on the hanger. Young women look great in them with just pearl or diamond stud earrings. On a mature woman, however, they must be made to the very highest standard by a genius if to be worn at all. Very little jewellery can be tolerated. You run the risk of looking overdone and vulgar. At the same time, beaded dresses have the incredible capacity to scream "Dowager Duchess" at any woman over fifty. If you love black glitter, buy a lightly beaded chiffon skirt to wear with a black cashmere sweater. Or, do the opposite with a beaded T-shirt and a knee-length satin pencil skirt or silk trousers. Add kitten-heeled black suede shoes, dark tights and a crocheted bag. Wear a taupe coloured silky trench coat over everything. This says *decontracté*, French for relaxed elegance.

Black silk or wool crepe palazzo pants take you everywhere from lunch to black tie. Beware, however, of black jersey if you have less than a perfect figure: though it is comfortable and stretchy, it tends to reveal every flaw. Palazzos in other fabrics can work for most bodies because they lengthen the leg and forgive. Check for any white spots always, and make a friend of your dry cleaner. Keeping black from looking grubby is very important. For the daytime wear a cream jersey T-shirt with a vintage paste necklace, a black or grey ribbed cardigan and a simple leather tie belt with your palazzo trousers. Complete the look with black boots and a Zoran or Shirin Guild assymetric jacket. For evening take the same trousers and match them with a black tuxedo jacket with satin lapels and a lace camisole underneath: wear with very high-heeled satin court shoes with diamante buckles. We love the look of a long chiffon coat floating over black satin. Wear your palazzo pants with a turtle-neck sweater and a cherry red embroidered satin coat.

Black MUSTS for your wardrobe:
• Well-cut trousers in all shapes: boot-leg, straight-cut, slightly flared, cigarette, cargo and low-waisted. Look for trousers that are made of heavy-gauge nylon. You can virtually wipe the spots off them with a kitchen cloth, which makes them ideal for travel. Since Miuccia Prada invented them, they are truly indispensable.
• A good black leather skirt: to wear with every fabric shirt, sweater or jacket, from cotton to denim, from silk to cashmere. Wear the skirt with a navy jacket to look almost like a suit but less formulaic. Add black suede boots with navy opaque tights and you have done what Jean Muir would have been doing if she were alive today. Never, *never* do the motorcycle dominatrix look of leather head to toe, unless you are into serious S&M. That look depends for its appeal on a young and innocent face, not a worldly one.
• A high-quality black leather jacket: the same rules of texture and cut apply. Try wearing one with a mottled grey tweed, A-line or printed black skirt in challis or viscose, with a low-slung belt. Keep it simple. Wear a black leather blazer, no studs please, with grey flannels or jeans and knot a fringed white silk man's evening scarf around your neck. When you wear a sweater underneath, try a shorter sleeve. It is cooler and encourages movement. Note: the better the leather, the more you pay for it, but the better the leather, the more comfortable it will be. Hang the expense, you will have it forever.
• Black suede boots (not patent leather because the matt finish is mini-mizing and classier unless, again, you are into the Belle de Jour look).
• Black high-heeled sling-back shoes: they look lighter and sexier than a court shoe.
• A sharp-cut calf-length cashmere coat. This is a basic for any woman. It is like a fur coat without the anxiety. You can wear it over anything. Just try to remember to wear something light and bright near the face – a lit-tle fur tippet, a colourful pashmina – because middle-aged skin is not quite as luminescent as it once was. Mix all this with flesh-coloured shoes and a quilted bag for a sophisticated change.

So What About Brown
Is brown the dull woman's version of black? We don't think so: it is the thinking woman's version of black. From a soft butter-brown leather bomber jacket with jeans to the bitter dark chocolates of Jil Sander in her heyday, brown has much to offer. It says rich earth, warmth, nature, boho,

arty, doesn't look too new and combines well with accents of acid colour. A glace brown leather skirt works beautifully with cream, grey, rust, camel and caramel. It gives great edge to pale blue, green and pink. What could be more stylish than brown trousers, matching sweater, a chartreuse green leather shoulder bag and vintage Daniel Hechter brown tweed jacket? If you try combining brown with black or navy, you'll be surprised at how chic brown can be. Brown checked suits are a classic fashion stalwart to wear in the day with leather shoes and in the night with brown velvet and silk shoes and a brown silk T-shirt. Brown means tweed, suede, leather, felt and fur, not to mention feathers – Philip Treacy has been known to do a fabulous hat in brown pheasant feathers, for the seriously chic.

Navy is a Workhorse

If black is rebellion and the avant-garde, and brown is cosy and familiar, then navy is authority and correctness. We love navy blue. Ever since nanny pushed us in our pram wearing a navy gabardine raincoat with her little graduation badge and beret we have been enamoured of navy. We cannot forget the sailor suits we wore as pre-teens and our gymslips! Nor can we forget those lovely little tweed coats with navy velvet collars we wore to school in winter. We look up to navy. Navy is someone reliable to watch over us. Navy is quality.

Think naval officers, airline pilots, bankers, police commissioners. Navy is an authoritative colour with a formality and seriousness that makes us trust it and those who wear it. Just ask any smartly turned-out self-respecting woman living in Geneva. They wouldn't think of going to a lunch without navy to fall back on. When we want to close a deal, hire someone, get our book published, meet the headmistress, chair a charity or run for political office, we look to navy blue. Deepest navy gives winter a lift, but try spicing it up with avocado-green accessories. Spring has sprung when the first navy-blue jackets hit the rails. They can look very pretty with mimosa or tangerine accessories. Try a pale-orange shell sweater and a large matching shawl. Navy is a true friend, very adaptable.

If you have olive skin and dark hair, navy is your best colour. Black will drain you. Navy will give light and clarity to your skin. If you are a blonde, assisted or natural, navy lights up your limpid blue or flashing green eyes. If you have dark skin, navy is less morbid than black and is a sharp dressy alternative. Navy is far less harsh than black but still does the same work. In a good quality fabric it tailors well. Think about a navy wool crêpe Jean Muir dress and jacket with a bit of smocking detail or a Jil Sander bias-cut wool voile dress for the cooler days of August.

For a totally non-seasonal look, try a navy pinstripe Ralph Lauren

trouser suit, with black high heels, a crisp white shirt and a Victorian silver chain and locket and a matching bangle. Carry a navy crocodile or
lizard clutch. Wear the same jacket with a skirt when you want to flash
your legs. Enjoy the contrast of sexy legs in high heels with pale hose
and the sharp conservatism of navy. Avoid pussycat bows at all costs.
Instead, try a scarf folded like a four-in-hand tie; this male-female thing
makes us feel more feminine. Wear a horizontal striped T-shirt with
navy and white in the spring. A narrow navy reefer coat makes a useful
alternative with skirts or trousers. Wear it with a navy skirt and a lilac-
grey blouse, tan belt, shoes and bag, and you have an instant suit. Giorgio
Armani always has a slim navy coat in his collections. Look for a two-
thirds-length double-breasted pea coat, preferably without brass buttons
(which look better on a commodore). Wear it with jeans, grey flannels or
cream trousers for that nautical feeling. Navy comes in any number of
shades from darkest midnight, almost black, to a medium blue called
French navy. All the great designers, Mainbocher, Chanel, Dior, St. Laurent, Armani and Hardy Amies, used masculine navy blue to emphasize
the extreme femininity of the women they adored.

Navy and white go together like gin and tonic; it is hard to imagine
one without the other, so clean and sharp. For your yacht it's a must!
Wear a short-sleeved navy cotton-knit sweater, white cropped linen
trousers, white ballet slippers and hoop earrings and you will summon
up images of Audrey Hepburn in *Sabrina Fair*, at least in your own mind.
Try a long-sleeved navy and white striped T-shirt with white drawstring
trousers and an orange cotton sweater knotted over your shoulders for
dinner by the sea. Pin a coral-red starfish brooch or a big enamel green
frog on your hip. Wear a white T-shirt and linen skirt with a buttonless
navy cardigan, pulled together with a big gold safety pin dangling a few
red bakelite cherries. Diana Vreeland would approve.

Colour Me

In the 1970s some clever person started a successful business of colour
counselling that put us all into categories: Summer, Winter, Spring and
Autumn. According to this theory, each season's woman was confined to
a certain colour palette. Winter was dark-haired, dark or very stark
white-skinned, brown eyed, and her allocated colours were black, red,
icy white and bright blue. It was a nice idea, but one couldn't help but
think that a fair-skinned brunette, otherwise known as Autumn, could
look just as good in these tones. A pale fragile blonde, Spring, should
only wear pastels, so went the theory. Red heads, another autumnal type,
could only wear shades of green, olive and rust. The Summer lady was
confined to yellows and oranges. Where is the logic of this colour fas-

cism, when so many of us change our hair colour at will and experiment with different-hued makeup?

If you have believed in it, now is the time to give it up. You can wear all the colours of the rainbow, as long as they are the right intensity for your skin and hair. There are some purples that can kill you dead, but there can be nothing more life-affirming than a bright-red violet. Some deep reds drain all the blood out of your face, but tomato and russet can give a flush to your cheeks. It is all in the shade, not the colour. Think about the many variations of white; there is a flattering white for just about everyone.

Pucci's multicolour patterns mixed burnt orange, cyclamen and chartreuse. Sonia Rykiel's hot pinks, dark greens, teal blues and striped beige-and-navy sweaters suited many complexions. We loved Christian Lacroix's circus-like explosions. Surely we didn't have to conform to one colour type or other to wear these wonderful inventive styles? Did you call your colour consultant when you were in the deep recesses of Rive Gauche? Of course not, because you were buying into a look, fashion, attitude, innovation and excitement. Your needs are no different now. You can use most colours to enliven and enrich whatever you are wearing. Just be aware of the power of colour near your face and adjust the intensity.

Some of today's combinations are simply too lurid for us. Harshly bright colours can be demanding and un-chic. We need to seek out the more subtle tones.

Yves St Laurent was an amazing colourist, and lessons can be still learned from his historic choices because he always designed for grown-up women. St Laurent combined bitter almond (a kind of musty pink) with avocado green or steel blue, so what about hot pink, sizzling red, Gitane blue and dazzling yellow? Just remember that you cannot do this top to bottom anymore. Learn to choose one striking thing – a jacket, coat, shirt, T-shirt –and leave it at that. Mix it with something neutral.

A few other thoughts on colour. If you have found a wonderful, multi-coloured Missoni-like sweater-coat and it sings to you, bring it down to earth by wearing it with jeans, khaki or chino trousers, grey sweat pants and low boots. Pick out one of the colours with a squashy hobo bag. When you mix several complementary colours the effect is oddly neutral. The colours counterbalance each other and the combination can virtually work like beige. If you are somewhat larger than you once were, don't drown yourself in dark colours. Taupe, off-white, cream, banana and silvery grey are complementary to most skin and hair and, spiked with bright colour, will make you look younger and livelier. You need not disappear into the woodwork. Whatever size you are, you are still a woman.

CHAPTER FIVE

Jeans Are Not for Teens

The Great Jeans Dilemma. Sociologists could write learned treatises on the place that blue jeans have occupied in our collective history. Jeans have become a sexual and social statement of considerable complexity and have to be analyzed in those terms. We, however, will attempt a simpler version.

Start with childhood. Jeans were camp, in the outdoors sense. Jeans were sporty, to go with tennis shoes and games. Jeans were for hiking. Jeans were for heavy, dirty jobs. Jeans were rebellion, rebel without a cause. Jeans were for slumming. You wore jeans when you went out for jazz or for pizza on the wrong side of town. Jeans were the guy that your father and mother hated. Jeans were for cleaning up the yard or the garage. Jeans were for chopping off into shorts. Essentially, jeans were for work, and they expressed a social attitude, a fashionable post-war left-wing solidarity with those who, through no fault of their own, did not belong to the bourgeoisie. Marilyn Monroe wore jeans in *The Misfits*; so did Arthur Miller watching from the wings. Janet Leigh wore rolled-up jeans. Jean Seberg wore jeans in *Breathless*. But jeans then were more an attitude than a way of life.

In the late 1960s jeans were rock 'n' roll: flared, bell-bottomed, ripped, stained, bleached, tie-dyed, patched, hip-hugging and shrunk. In the 1970s you had to lie down on the floor to pull them on. Commentators even feared for our fertility. Rock 'n' roll had made jeans sexy, and from sexy they became erotic, complete with chains, belts, crosses, skulls and bones, bondage ties and endless studs.

Jeans have always been anti-establishment, but today they are the establishment's uniform as well. No wonder there are so many cuts and brands out there competing for position. Everyone wants a unique pair to express something about herself. Jeans have assumed an aspect of our fashion lives so complex that it is hard to know why you wear them, how to wear them, and what it means when you do. But wear them we must.

First and foremost, jeans are about youth. When were we at our most rebellious? When we were young. And how long does that last? Although the money still belongs to youth's elders, jeans are worn by those who seek to fit into a contemporary society that values only youthful beauty. And how do we differentiate between the still young and those who would desire to *seem* young? Jeans manufacturers produce a wide spectrum of styles that radically differentiate social status and age. Only teenagers with the firmest flesh can successfully sport the very low-slung, nearly pubis-baring jeans of recent years. The younger the wearer, the louder the message, and the lower the jeans are worn. Suitable accoutrements to this statement are cropped sweaters and see-through lingerie look-alike tops that reveal the mid-section, the belly-button jewel or the less-than-tasteful tattoo. By now done to death, the very low-slung jean looks frightful and slovenly on anyone who isn't perfect. Even if you have exercised your stomach to a washboard, had a tummy tuck and a buttock lift, your hands and face will give you away immediately. Do not feel you have to wear jeans like these.

So why wear jeans at all? Are you doing heavy cleaning, getting under your car to fix the exhaust pipe or taking long country walks through piles of mulch and barbed-wire fencing? Are you deathly afraid of being spotted as a grown up with a certain level of income? These are good reasons, but not the only ones. Most of us are susceptible to the siren call of appearing young and competing sexually. And there are practical reasons for jeans: they are comfortable and don't wrinkle. They are great at the desk, in the car and sitting on an airplane. They are an indestructible uniform. Jeans can and should be worn by a woman over fifty, if she so desires, but there are a few rules to bear in mind.

Jeans are sexy when they are snug, and they should be snug. There is nothing more middle-aged and desperate than jeans that are cut to look like loose trousers. The baggy hip-hop look, very effective as a ghetto-fabulous youth image, is not for us. Your jeans must be cut for your shape. Consider the rear-end view first, last and foremost. Your derrière is what jeans are about, along with the length of your legs.

Go to any good jeans emporium, check out the newest brands and try every cut to see what suits you. Our favourites include Seven for all Mankind, Citizens of Humanity and Rock and Republic. Why? Because they fit. Jeans must fit across the rear, so buy a larger size if necessary and have the waist band adjusted. Or, just keep looking until you find the brand for you, and stick to it. Wear your jeans with mid- to high-heeled boots or shoes to add length to the leg. Never shorten your own jeans. They must be cut off properly and stitched. There is nothing cruder than a homemade hem. And as a rule, do not buy jeans with holes. Okay, you can have one strategically placed little hole on a pocket or at the knee, but remember how fast one chic little hole can spread into a massive rent and make you look like you have been shopping for cast-offs.

What to wear with your jeans? Like other items of clothing, jeans do change with the seasons. In autumn and winter, dark jeans look good with fitted black turtle-neck sweaters and long tweed coats. In summer you can wear pale-blue washed-out jeans with a white T-shirt or a linen shirt with a Western-style beaded belt. Jeans look good with a blazer, a leather jacket or a brightly coloured cardigan with a diamante button. Make your jeans look feminine with a bit of detailing and jewellery. There is nothing cooler than a well-fitted pair of jeans, a smart twin set and pearls, with boots in the winter and sandals in the summer. Though it is a bit of a cliché by now, a serious jacket with your well-cut jeans and high heels is always a good look. Try a velvet or embroidered satin coat with your jeans for a fun look at lunch in a trendy restaurant. Thread your folded Hermès scarf through the loops, instead of a belt or chain, when wearing your Barbour. Accessorize your denim look with vintage costume brooches, turquoise and coral beads and woven leather belts and shoes.

Wash your jeans carefully in cold water and let them dry naturally; do not put them in the dryer. Dry-clean them if you are worried about shrinkage. Iron your jeans by all means, but never iron in creases. Dirty, soiled or sat-out jeans are for artists, workers, rock stars of a certain age, fifteen-year-olds and mountain walkers.

Black Jeans – Unless you are an architect or engineer, we would avoid these. They fade to grey at the first washing and thereafter look a bit dirty. If we can't dissuade you, team them with a Navajo silver conch belt and a black or cream silk shirt. A real conch belt might cost upwards of £2500 at Ralph Lauren, but if your travels take you to the American West to Wyoming, keep an eye out for one there. Otherwise, forget the whole thing.

White Jeans – For summer only, white jeans are funky and fun, especially ones woven with a bit of stretch, if you have a good figure. Something about them says less "seashore" than the usual white linen or cotton trousers. Cut narrowly they look neat and appropriate on a bright day with silver and turquoise Indian jewellery and a tobacco-coloured suede jacket. On a grey day, nothing quite catches the eye like white jeans, a short black leather jacket, black silk sweater and amber beads. Add a cute pair of Minnie Mouse wedges, and you have the ideal summer-in-the-city look.

As with everything else you wear, update your jeans from time to time. The newest leg or waist will modernize your whole look. Beware, however, of any brand that pushes the high-waisted look. Unless you are over six feet tall, skinny as a snake with absolutely no flesh around your middle, you will find these impossible to wear comfortably. Worse, they will shorten your waist, lengthen your bottom and chop off your legs. Disaster.

CHAPTER SIX

Speaking of Blazers

You wore them to school, complete with a badge. You hated them and longed for a pink angora sweater with shiny buttons. (You should have both in your wardrobe, though maybe baby pink is not as appropriate as it once was.) Perhaps it has become a cliché, but a blazer is an indispensable component of the stylish wardrobe, something you can pull out with confidence again and again. In navy-blue or black, in wool, cashmere, silk, linen, cotton or velvet, the blazer hides figure flaws and lends authority, just as it does for men. It can become a virtual body for you, if the tailoring and fit are right. It makes a timeless back-drop for a stunning piece of antique jewellery. Now is the moment for that heirloom piece.

Picture this: you are late for lunch with the architect who is design-ing your loft conversion. You need to impress. You wear straight-cut, grey flannel trousers over low-heeled boots, pistachio-green ribbed sweater, dark navy blazer, big cameo brooch, chunky watch (so you can see the time) and peridot drop earrings. Add a multicoloured scarf and some crocheted driving gloves. You look in charge. Not so bourgeois that no one can relate to you, but smart and a little funky.

Short and boxy blazers are good for skinny ladies with narrow hips because they appear to lengthen the legs. Long, narrow-waisted blazers disguise ample bosoms and wider hips. Look for blazers with minimal padding and structure. You do not need a landing-pad-size shoulder, just a soft and touchable fabric with a pristine cut. For a bit of erotic charge, you can wear a blazer with nothing underneath except a lace bra and

Chanel no. 5. This is your opportunity to wear your pearls, a dramatic-animal or diamond-bow brooch in a sporty way, or an armful of bangles. If you wear your blazer with a navy-and-white polka-dot chiffon blouse and a knee-length grey flannel skirt you are talking business, but if you wear your blazer with a simple white shirt and jeans, you convey a relaxed air and youth along with it. Quality, however, is everything. Buy the best blazer you can afford. It can take you anywhere.

Don't be frightened of buying a red blazer. In fact, go for it. A red leather blazer from Franck Namini on the Rue de Rivoli in Paris is a luxury item that will pay for itself in chic many times over.

CHAPTER SEVEN

The Cult of the T-Shirt

D o you remember seeing, back in the early 1970s, the issue of *Vogue* with Lauren Hutton on the cover – all gap-toothed smile, swingy loose hair, blue jeans, white deck shoes and *the* T-shirt – pronouncing that the homely white garment was the building block of every woman's wardrobe? She was the quintessential image of the post-swinging Sixties, when the mini-skirt and Twiggy had taken the imagination by the throat and replaced the woman with the woman-child. Hutton, however, was certainly not childlike. She was fully a woman, and she represented a new beauty template. Her look was sporty, natural, even boyish and very informal. The image of child-woman-boy, all wrapped up in a single image, is still with us today.

Along with that image, the lowly T-shirt has remained on the fashion agenda. Once only found in men's underwear departments, the T-shirt today has been elevated to an art, a cult, a way of life. More than an option, it has become a necessity and an essential part of every wardrobe. For the middle-aged woman, it can be a new best friend. But what to do if you are no longer shaped like Twiggy, or your curves are far more ample than Lauren Hutton's? Are you more Oprah than Beyonce? Here are some good rules.

First, foremost and always: NO LOGOS. If you are an adult female, there is no reason whatsoever to wear a T-shirt inscribed with a message (unless you happen to own shares in a national football club, brewery or are promoting your own business). As Fran Lebowitz, the well-known writer for *The New Yorker* magazine stated in her amusing book, *Metropol-*

itan Life, she didn't especially want to hear from *you*, so why would she want to hear from your T-shirt? Since the 1980s, when the political activist–designer Katherine Hammett produced a range of provocative logos, T-shirt literature has lost its iconic value. Stella McCartney has revived an unimaginative take on the printed T-shirt, and if you think that running around with the word "BRISTOLS" on your front is amusing, then we cannot help you. Other subscribers to this genre include Paul Smith, John Galliano, Giorgio Armani and almost everyone else. The comic strip image is not for the middle-aged so do not even go there. In short, no T-shirts that say anything to do with sex, skulls, movie stars, drugs, cute aphorisms, brand names, quotes from poems and definitely nothing that says "fcuk."

The only exception to this rule is when you are lying on your bed, alone, eating crisps and watching television, or on the beach. Do wear one around the house as an occasional, ironic comment to your grown-up children, to let them know that mother is still conscious.

Let Us Talk About Arms

Almost everyone complains about underarm flab, loss of tone and fat. There is of course some wear and tear over time. Skin gets looser, a bit wrinkly and underarm areas can appear to "overflow." Arms, like legs, are genetically inherited from someone else. You can do one hundred tricep curls a day, swim forty laps and still have some flab (especially if your mother or aunt has some too). What can we do about this?

This brings us to sleeves. T-shirts, whatever the price range, come in a variety of styles: sleeveless, cap-sleeved, short or slanted, tight, loose, three-quarters, long and flapping beyond your wrists. You may not like the sight of your upper arms, but the choice of sleeve can improve your self-image. You could buy a sleeveless or short-sleeved model and wear it under your jackets, cardigans or an open shirt. It will allow comfortable movement, look young and chic, and keep you cool. If you want to go sleeveless in the summer without a cover-up, just liberate yourself and DO IT. If you are overly concerned, throw a gauzy scarf over your shoulders and walk tall. A nice sleeve for the more self-conscious is the three-quarter-length sleeve, or try pushing longer sleeves up to your elbows for a casual look. You can show off your pretty watch, a charm bracelet or row of bakelite bangles on your wrists and forearms. The sainted Jean Muir always cut her sleeve lengths on the shorter side to highlight chunky jewellery.

The White T-Shirt

Like the crisp white cotton shirt, the white T-shirt is always appropriate.

It refers to youth, it multitasks, goes with everything, can be worn day and night and, if properly cared for, can last through any number of washes. It looks chic under a tailored suit. It 'works out' in the gym. It imparts insouciance to any outfit and can actually make something starchy and middle-aged look much more with it. It must, however, be well cut for your body shape.

If you have a bosom, skin-tight T-shirts are out. You are not the age for this, and it always looks cheap. Try to find a shape that fits close but skims the body, that shows off your feminine figure without binding it. Look for a weight of cotton that is not too transparent, as anything too flimsy will appear inelegant, especially if what is revealed is less than perfect. Opaque white in a good cut is chic, particularly with a bit of jewellery at the neck. Avoid ribbed effects as they emphasize the wrong aspects on a larger woman's body. Stay away from anything fussy, such as Dolce & Gabbana's corset T-shirts, with their hooks, eyes, medallions of the Madonna and Child and ribbons hanging everywhere. These are expensive, wishful-thinking items and belong to the second-tier celebrity set.

You can find white T-shirts in all price ranges. Some of the best are made by Banana Republic in the U.S.A. They are well cut, have a nice, hollowed-out neckline and attractive short sleeves cut on a slant. The cotton is high quality – not too thick, not too transparent, and it launders well. T-shirts made by the Gap are also good, although sometimes the cotton can be a bit too heavy and does not wash as well as other brands. The popular manufacturer Michael Stars makes basic T-shirts in every possible style. Look out for them in the jeans sections of department stores, or visit Bloomingdale's website. The Italian label, Diesel, is another good source. As the major chains continue to research fabrics – improving and expanding their penetration of the market – there is little doubt that even better T-shirts are on the way.

Too much lycra in a T-shirt, for example, is not a good thing; this material should carry a warning. Although it can be a useful addition to many fabrics, such as cotton and wool to help them retain their shape, it has its problems. In excess, lycra does all the wrong things. It washes badly, becomes rough to the touch, pills, shrinks, bunches up and is uncomfortable and hot. Lycra does few favours for the larger-breasted woman, at least when she is out of the gym.

The designer T-shirt is fine if you must have one, but considering the money you have to fork out, it is not as wonderful as it should be. Agnes B. makes a great shaped T-shirt, but the fabric tends to roughen after a few washes. Jil Sander's T-shirts are even more expensive, and can appear awkwardly shaped for anyone not in the form of an ironing board. With his miniature Polo-playing logos, Ralph Lauren is famous for his T-shirts, but they cost the earth. Prada's T-shirts have a good fit and a bit of wit, with their distressed cotton fabrics and interesting applied motifs, but again, you are paying top prices (and they frequently require dry-cleaning because of their extra detailing and delicacy). Marni's T-shirts are wonderfully soft and luminous, made of the thinnest cotton, but they require that you have no midriff whatsoever because the slightest bulge will be on show. John Smedley has an excellent range of cotton T-shirts that he produces each season. We love the short-sleeved, longer bodied styles with rounded necks – they work with just about everything and wash like a dream. Wolford makes a stretchy T-shirt, but, again, you must check for unwelcome bulges.

More generally, a few more thoughts: a round-necked T-shirt accommodates a necklace, pearls, brooch or scarf. Avoid straight lines, à la boat-necks, as these tend to be too severe. V-necks are pretty and elongating as long as they do not reveal too much cleavage. If you are worried about the skin on your neck, wear a little chiffon or silk scarf tied into a neat little knot. Halter-neck T-shirts can be fabulous if you have good shoulders and upper arms.

What you wear under a T-shirt also bears consideration. Smooth nylon or cotton bras are best. Lace may be a little too transparent for modesty, and cause a crinkly effect. Never buy a padded T-shirt bra – you see them everywhere, shaped like giant breakfast bowls and they make you look twice your size. They push everything up, out or sideways and basically negate the whole purpose of the smooth, unencumbered line. Let us repeat: unsupported, flabby flesh under a T-shirt is not a pretty sight. And never, ever wear an over-sized T-shirt – NOT EVEN IN BED – and never with leggings. This option disguises nothing. It is shapeless, unflattering, unfeminine, reeks of insecurity and is downright off-putting.

One final tip for keeping your T-shirts in good order: washing machine, yes; drier, never (unless you want to down size with every cleaning).

The T-shirt Subset
The white T-shirt is best because it is classic, useful, easiest to keep clean and brings the most light to our faces. Do not deviate from it unless you have to. From time to time, however, here are some alternatives but bear the following in mind:

Black is beautiful because it is urban. It does not show grime, looks good with everything, is minimizing and smart. It goes well with all kinds of ethnic and decorative accessories, and looks fine dressed up or down. To keep a black T-shirt in pristine order, never launder it in the washing machine. Keep it separate from all other colours and fabrics, and dry it flat – never in a dryer. This way you avoid the inevitable lint problem and fading. Navy-blue is good but not for everyone. It looks best when you have some colour in your face, and is deadly when you are pale. Black is always better.

Khaki is a nice colour on virtually everyone because it brings out the pink in your skin and looks interesting. It goes well with white, black, red, orange, pink and is a basic travel colour. Wear a khaki T-shirt with a pair of beige cargo trousers, linen drawstring pants, white jeans, black silk palazzos, wrap-around jersey or linen skirt. Khaki is great in the summer, with ivory or gold jewellery. Forget beige or tan – white is better.

Say yes to pastels if they are worn in the south of France or Italy at a smart resort with matching coloured, beautifully cut jeans, or with plain linen or cotton Capri pants. Choose the pastel shade that looks best on you and wear it simply with flat sandals, no jewellery and a straw bag. But, remember, white is always better. Pastels fade. Under no circumstances should you wear strong, solid colours. They wash badly, lose their colour immediately and are harsh in the light.

No patterns, dots, opticals, stripes or floral sprigs. One notable exception, however, is the Pucci T-shirt in silk or cotton, with its flamboyant, psychedelic patterns in rainbow colours. These must be worn in the simplest of ways, that is, no jewellery, little makeup and flattish shoes. Through their next generation of designers, Missoni has had a new lease of life and now make T-shirts in the most lovely Bargello patterns and earthy colours that are flattering and gorgeous and not for children. Missoni says a bit about your mind with its haute-bohemian quality.

CHAPTER EIGHT

Bohemian Rhapsody

Forget your old ideas about ethnic costume. Interesting fabrics, styles and jewellery can help you find a new self in a way that is neither overly tailored or formal. An ultra-fashionable Italian friend finds inspiration from Chinese jackets, batik skirts, Tunisian jewellery, printed pashminas, ponchos and eccentric hats. She used to dress head-to-toe in Armani, which looked great before she turned sixty. She was very tailored, with just a bit of eccentricity in her accessories. As her fashion language evolved, she began adding more exotic notes, pairing her classic look with items from the Near and Far East. She added fur trim and vintage shawls to give interest to what she already had in her cupboards. She doesn't replace things every season, but uses what she has with imagination. We particularly love her knitted hats and ample squashy embellished handbags.

At night, another Latin friend wears either black or brown skinny trousers with chunky boots, and a long velvet jacket with a fur scarf, on which she pins a giant jewelled iguana. She too has a collection of antique silver tribal jewellery and yards of Murano glass beads. Although not beautiful, she has the flair and confidence to put together a highly individual look with a few striking pieces. Both these women have opted for an alternative, less branded identity. The key is proportion and quality of design. Look around; stare at other women. Let your eye adjust to new ways of wearing old things. Experiment in front of the mirror. Bohemia has been a hot look on the high streets for young girls. We are not suggesting a spangled skirt, off-the-shoulder peasant blouse and Ugg boots, but we do advocate a more sparing, selective approach to wearing funky pieces.

First, be certain that the colours suit your skin tones. Traditional fabrics from the East tend to be a little strident to the Western eye, so you must be on the lookout for the less obvious colour combinations. Read the fashion columns in newspapers for new trends in accessories, but keep in mind that stylists are there to make photographs look good, not necessarily to give a realistic assessment of the product. There are always articles in the press about Bohemian style, whether high or low. Young models, rarely older than sixteen, are swathed in yards of drooping chiffon, mohair sweaters and trailing scarves, dripping fake crystals and feathers and generally made up to look like ghostly bag ladies. The stylist loads them down with everything from high-button shoes to hair extensions, essentially because individually the items are so boring. There is little for you to learn from this, except the following: do not try this, even at home. Keep it simple.

Wear a shawl, perhaps in fringed caramel suede, a long pair of amber earrings and matching boots with a neat black skirt and sweater and some antique silver bracelets for a slightly Country and Western look. Try an antique-style paisley shawl with chunky bakelite bangles and a Prada plastic chain belt, and you have an entirely different look. Put on a black brocade jacket over jeans or a black pair of trousers. Tie at the waist with a leather string belt and sport some Victorian jet-drop earrings.

A little goes a long way. Smart London and New York women go to fashion fairs or look through the weekend section of newspapers for tiny, out-of-the-way shops for inspiration. Caution: Brick Lane in East London is brilliant for chapattis and samosas, and you can have lunch and buy fantastic sticky sweets, but it is not generally a good source for exotic fashion accessories. It would be better to do your trawling in the Edgware Road. Always look for the highest quality of materials and workmanship, remembering that you are not doing a feature for the *National Geographic* magazine on tribalism. You are using ethnic accents in a stylish way to enhance what is essentially Western dress.

A touch of the exotic brings things into sharper perspective. We know a woman who wore black nylon trousers, a black polo-necked jersey and a short black-and-silver kimono jacket with two 1930s sapphire clips who looked chic and relaxed. She had taken basic items, mixed them with something Japanese, some period jewellery, and produced a look that was unique and timeless. On the other hand, another woman we know, apparently trying to achieve a similar effect, came dressed as none other than Pandit Nehru in a flowing beige silk tunic, leggings à la

Mahatma Ghandi, and a sari-like shawl tossed over one shoulder. She wore Indian jewels and matching moccasins. She looked neither chic nor authentic. An Indian or Pakistani woman of the same age wearing the identical outfit would have looked as if she were honouring her culture and background. A Western woman going for the full costume looks as if she is auditioning for a bit part in *A Passage to India*. However much you might adore the styles of India, Japan, Arabian nights or Mexican hat dancers never indulge in the whole look outside a fancy-dress evening or costumed event. Use ethnic dressing as you would a spice. Taste for another culture's treasures is seasoning, not the whole meal.

Where should you find inspiration? Whenever you go on a business trip or holiday to a far-flung place, look for local crafts: bags, belts, skirts, hats, trinkets, shoes. For example, each region in Mexico offers different traditional embroidered blouses and dresses. Wear one over a bathing suit or cropped trousers with a raffia belt. Carved-bone necklaces and pairs of papier mâché bracelets are charming. Tooled leather from Morocco and traditional woven sarongs from Indonesia have an authentic look that can add special flavour. But beware of wearing a caftan as a dress over jeans, unless you are prepared to look like an unmade bed; they work better in the bedroom or on the beach. Avoid the expensive silk jacket cut by a "tent-maker." Often found in pushy tourist traps, these things have little shape and are essentially unwearable once you get them home. Everyone fondly remembers those Moroccan slippers in tobacco suede that you thought were so chic until you actually tried to walk in them; without any kind of heel you felt as if you were tipping over backwards. And how can we forget the expensive silk caftan with the artful macramé buttoning system that went the full length of the garment? The merchant forgot to mention that once undone, these devilish little buttons would never refastened. We all make mistakes – but try to cut your losses and learn what will actually work for you.

Beware of cheap carved soapstone or nasty faux-jade trinkets that are mass produced in Hong Kong and Singapore. Though our tastes may be different, what is valuable in the West is equally so in the East. There is no substitute for quality, no matter where you visit. You can, however, find excellent local designers who create unique pieces in their own cultural idiom, and these are always worth buying. If you have a favourite suit that you've considered having copied on a jaunt through Southeast Asia, remember that there is a good reason why tailoring is so expensive in the Western world. Experience, expertise and taste, not just a sewing machine, make a garment wearable. Certainly, there are some good tailors, but insist on several fittings and take more time than just a day to have something made. In the Far East the best buys are good jade, lengths of silk, fine linen handkerchiefs and embroidered shawls.

One recent source of fashion treasure is in mysterious Argentina, home of political unrest, beef, the tango and mountains of leather goods, which range from the cheap and crude to the soft, creamy and utterly desirable. Don't be misled by price alone. Feel every bag, every jacket and look at the more upmarket choices. Even the most expensive pieces are an incredible bargain. How many times have we returned home with a bag full of coarsely made, brittle and cheaply coloured items, only to give them away? Whatever you find, add each piece sparingly to your wardrobe. A little goes a long way.

CHAPTER NINE

Vintage

O ne of our favourite fashions today is something people call "vintage," equating something drinkable on a world scale that has improved with age to what are really just old clothes. A distinction must be made between antique, vintage, second-hand and used clothes.

"Antique" usually refers to clothes made before the turn of the twentieth century and reflects a world before two earth-shattering wars. They were usually worn by upper-class women and required corsets, petticoats and a lady's maid to get it all on. The best of these costumes are now found in museums, but antique lingerie shops in London like Lunn's in the King's Road or Virginia in Portland Place sell, as well as copy, the underclothing of those bygone styles. There you can find camisoles, shirts and old-fashioned nightgowns. A pretty antique petticoat can make a stunning summer skirt with a white cotton-knit sweater, tan leather belt and sandals. Most antique outerwear, if available at all, would be too fragile to wear and unusable today except as fancy dress – and it would be considerably smaller.

"Vintage" should refer almost exclusively to haute couture, sewn by hand and designed by such great couturiers as Dior, St. Laurent, Mainbocher, Jacques Fath, Balenciaga, Fortuny, Madame Grès (also known as Alix) Lanvin, Balmain and Chanel – names that are generally collected as works of art. Rare and very expensive, they have been snapped up by collectors and dealers. These days vintage also connotes a fashion choice of well-made, off-the-peg clothing from past prêt-à-porter collections by these same designers. Fashion editors encourage their readers to mix new and vintage for a "customized" style.

Vintage Redux

Let us get one thing straight. In our opinion, there is no such thing as smart vintage unless it is from couture, was inherited from your mother or is made of antique fabric from the Orient. What passes as vintage for the young are just old clothes for the over-fifties. Vintage are the things you already have in your own closet and are reluctant to part with, perhaps for sentimental reasons. Vintage might be an exchange you made with a friend, but it is no longer chic and was never going to be on you.

With the demise of haute couture philosophy in the 1970s, the only way young students of fashion could find inspiration and learn technique was by looking at designer clothes in second-hand shops, literally taking them apart to understand their construction. At the same time, good design became less wearable, and young working women looked less to current fashion, which was mostly crazy and out of their price range, and more to previous decades for clothes and ornament. Thus the idea of vintage as a style was born.

Vintage was a return to femininity and quality. Vintage fulfilled young women's desire to have something unique while combining it with pieces of cheaper, more basic clothing. The more knowing practitioners of this art of combining created a rather ironic style. As an initial reaction to this, at the retail end, were labels that merely recycled poor garments into incredibly expensive designs. What might have come out of a Salvation Army rag bag was embellished with velvet ribbons and glitter into high style. To heighten the irony, some shops even demanded club cards to gain access. Their success led others to search through racks and bins of discards, and to copy this look in cheaper and equally funky alternatives – a little trim here, an antique button there, distressed devore velvets, suddenly a whole new style was born. The second-hand shops saw the trend and simply renamed their recycled clothes "vintage."

When designers are bereft of ideas, they tend to use irony as a substitute for creative imagination. They deconstruct and regurgitate a version of past glories, without the technical and sociological understanding of the originals. Avid fashion-seekers long for a past when the qualities of production provided elegance of fit and colour. It is not surprising that a few years ago Julia Roberts showed up to the Oscars in a classic Valentino dress. It had style and grace, and while wearing it, so did she.

Large manufacturers as well as resale shops have jumped on this trend. It is amusing to see Etro advertising some of their recent lines as vintage. In this case, as in others, vintage is really retro – using past ideas in current design production. All fashion, all art, is essentially referential, but in the case of retro, it is simply copying. There is no adjustment to the present time, no novelty or originality. It is a clone of the past and a dead-end. When you see a real fashion throw-back in the shops, remember that you probably wore that same style when you were thirty-five.

Is there any time that the mature woman can use vintage for herself? Yes, if you have a classically cut piece that was terribly expensive, went out of style the moment you bought it and was put away for safe keeping. For example, an old cashmere Hermès riding jacket with a velvet collar and leather tabs, or an evening gown made specially by a great designer. Useful vintage possibilities might be an exquisitely beaded jacket without shoulder pads to be worn with a matching new chiffon pair of trousers, or a hippy-styled fur coat from the 1970s. If you happen across a wonderful crocodile or lizard handbag in the antique markets, and the condition is great, you should buy it. The modern equivalent will cost ten times the price. Anything from Chanel can be kept and re-introduced to the wardrobe because these are always iconic pieces and because there is a certain kind of snobbery to old Chanel that says "I had it before you even knew the location of the shop." But if the threads are pulled and the shoulders are wrong, sell it. Someone will love it.

Old couture is always an exception to this rule. One friend was given a trunk full of Hartnell masterpieces by her mother. She had them properly cleaned, repaired and refitted and wears them whenever the occasion demands. You need a sense of adventure and self-confidence for this. Meanwhile, if you like a challenge and a good day out with a friend in London, visit Virginia, Cornucopia, Liberty's and antique markets such as Gray's for high-quality vintage buys. Christie's South Kensington has regular clothes auctions and for collectors they are a must.

"Second-Hand Rose"

Rich women have always recycled their wardrobes when the new season hits. Jackie Kennedy was reputed to have sold her clothes at the Ritz Thrift Shop in New York in order to buy new ones. Today, there are many second-hand clothes dealers who sell medium- to high-quality, nearly-new clothes that are desirable and relatively inexpensive compared to those in the shops. We see young and not-so-young women regularly scanning the racks for almost-new, high-fashion clothing at affordable prices. Second hand is not, however, to be confused with vintage, although the lines can sometimes be blurred. A beautiful Pucci or Hermès printed silk blouse (or possibly a Chanel suit) certainly qualifies as vintage because although they were machine made, the quality of their production remains high. On the whole, however, second-hand is good for us because we can sell the things we no longer want, and enjoy the experience of making room in our cupboards for something new and fresh, not to mention useful.

NOT
CLOTHES

CHAPTER TEN

The Joys of Jewellery

What does jewellery really mean? What do we say about ourselves when we adorn our bodies with metal and stones? We can get a hint of its significance by analyzing the tribal aspects of jewellery.

First and foremost, it was and is a repository of value. Indian women are given trousseaus of gold, elaborately worked necklaces, head pieces, nose rings, earrings, anklets and bracelets, which they wear on their wedding day. It is an expression of their social value, as well as decoration. It indicates their status as part of a family in a traditional culture. Italian women of a certain class are given valuable jewellery to wear as they marry, for many of the same reasons: status, position, identity, self-esteem, an expression of worldly wealth and adornment. North African women express their tribal ties and status with intricate silver necklaces, amulets, bracelets and earrings. American women flash their diamond solitaires; Park Avenue ladies who lunch wear giant chunks of gold and stones courtesy of David Webb and Seaman Schepps to declare their position.

In other words, whether you are Western or Eastern, jewellery sends a number of important personal, social and global messages. The large diamond solitaire is not so much a fashion statement as a symbol of security, pride, ownership and even studied vulgarity. What about the small and intriguing antique carved signet ring? What does that say about someone? Does it mean that she cannot afford something flashier, or that she prefers to reject ostentation? Is it a personal talisman, a good luck charm? Is it sentimental? What do multitudes of rings, stacks of little chains and teensy earrings communicate about the person wearing them? What do head-lamp-sized, clip-on earrings express about your personality? Not a lot, except that you may be stuck in a time warp. When you reach a certain age and status, and you have some money to spend, you have more choices about how and what you want to say about yourself. Do you want to change your look?

You can come up with something far more stylish, but you need to clear your mind of old habits as well as your jewellery box. Go through your collections of real and faux and isolate the things you most love and keep those handy. You enjoy them, and they make you feel special. Wear them often and don't put them away for only special occasions. You are here in the now, and now it is time to wear your favourites. Try on everything you have, even those bits and pieces tucked in the back of your top drawer. Take the things that no longer suit you, or bore you, and give them away or send them to auction. If that seems too drastic, put them in a safe place and forget about them. Talk to a jeweller you trust to reset some old stones or repair anything that is damaged. A good stone in an Edwardian ring might look better reset on a short chain or in a thick gold sportier ring. Convert necklaces into bracelets if there might be more use for them. A thorough clear-out makes the mind think more creatively.

Earrings are always good for the ego, but as a woman gets older, the size of the earring should vary inversely with her age. During the day, smaller earrings or none at all are younger, hence better. Dangling earrings are more casual and funkier; their movements when you toss your hair make you feel youthful. In the evening you might try some antique cut-steel earrings or rock crystals that sparkle like diamonds but are easier (and safer) to wear. They have a softer glow, as do rough-cut Indian diamonds. People will ask you about them. Do some research on the internet and recount the history of nineteenth-century metal-casting and the healing powers of crystal. At the very least, you will have a new topic of conversation.

We have mixed opinions about **pearls,** though many of us have selections of chokers, long and short strands, double- and triple-strand necklaces, real and fake. Pearls have a beautiful glow and are flattering on any skin. They soften and illuminate your face. But they can also make you look dowdy if you insist on wearing them only in the traditional ways. London jeweller Kiki McDonough suggests wearing your best white pearls with jeans and sweaters. Wear coloured pearls and pearl-and-stone combinations for dressing up in the evening. Quirky colours and unexpected contrasts are more interesting, will invite comment and update your look. You can wear your creamy pearls with a black sweater and trousers when you want to be more dressed up without trying too hard. Wear pearls as a belt at the waist – Chanel always did.

Pearl chokers can age you, especially with that wonderful Edwardian clasp you inherited from your Aunt Sally. You might wear one in a more lighthearted way, perhaps tucked in the neckline of a trouser suit or a white silk shirt with black trousers, but never with your cocktail dress. Even better, convert the clasp into a brooch and the pearls into a lariat with a large pearl or stone at either end or as a long swingy rope. If you adore your Edwardian clasp and cannot bear to part with it, transform it into a glorious pink- or grey-pearl bracelet. River pearls are not expensive and have a great casual look.

Brooches

It is well known that in recent years few people have understood the value of a good brooch. Traditionally, the brooch was worn on the shoulder of a suit, complete with a stiff coiffure and a triple strand of pearls. It can be a good grown-up look, particularly if you are being inaugurated as a Lady Mayor but not appropriate for our purposes. A diamond brooch is elegant, expensive and classy-looking. Diamond brooches are serious stuff. If you have one, or if you have seen one that you want, try dressing it down by wearing it in a more capricious way, perhaps with grey flannel trousers and a jeans jacket from Dolce & Gabbana. Fasten it on a fur scarf. Pin it on an unexpected place – the waist, the hip, or to hold your buttonless Marni cardigan in place. In other words, make it relevant to today by relaxing the use of it.

There is far more to brooches than just diamonds. They come in many sizes, shapes and materials. Cast your eyes over any antique jewellery counter, and you will be amazed by the inventiveness of the Victorians and Edwardians. Jewellery designed in the 1920s and 1930s is among the finest ever made in terms of craftsmanship. Why not wear a Victorian seed-pearl bow brooch at your throat instead of a gold chain, or, better still, mount it on a velvet handbag or beret. You can wear an enamelled silver Art Nouveau brooch by Liberty & Co. smack dab in the middle of your pullover. Fasten your brooch on a silk or leather cord and wear it as a necklace or a belt. Wear brooches in pairs. Wear two or three unmatching but similar-sized brooches on your blazer lapel.

A few practical considerations: if you pin a brooch to lightweight fabric, such as taffeta or silk, place a small square of cotton underneath to anchor it and prevent ripping. Never attach your brooch to your bra underneath. We invariably forget we have done it and untold damage can be the unhappy result when you whip off your sweater. Be aware that countless metal piercings of white silk or cashmere often lead to a dart-board look.

Fake jewellery – or what the French call "*fantasie*" – can be inspirational. We love big, dramatic fakes, not little wannabes. Chanel, Monet, Trifari, Schiaparelli, Dior and Pellini, to mention a few, made great pieces that you can find in antique and flea markets. Swarowski make beautiful crystal flowers and insects today, and somewhat cheaper versions can be found at Butler & Wilson on London's Fulham Road. Basia Zarzycka, whose Aladdin's cave–like shop is off Sloane Square in London's Chelsea, is a most creative designer specializing in fake and semi-precious jewels and icons. Amid a plethora of fabulous silk net scarves, vintage-look evening bags, handmade shoes and artificial flowers, you will find some of the most original drop earrings in town. Everything in her shop is unique and has enormous style.

Beware, however, of fakes that aspire to look like the real thing, which copy gemstones facet for facet. No one will be fooled when you appear in a 12-carat canary diamond that is really a zircon, and, if they are, you will spend far too much time explaining where you got it and how. The point of faux is not to ape the original but to create something new and beautiful out of non-precious materials. A friend, Italian of course, wears very blatant fakes, large shocking-pink or acid-green chandelier-size earrings at night with matching cashmere scarves. Combined with plain black trousers and a black T-shirt with Che Guevara's image, she never fails to draw attention.

Many of us have collections of good jewellery that we have accumulated through the years. Remember, styles change even in the classics, and a good rule of thumb is what Chanel advocated at least seventy years ago: put fake and real together. Wear real as if it were fake and fake as if it were real. Wear your diamonds with jeans, and wear fabulous fakes with an evening gown. Mix it up. Buy something crazy and wonderful from time to time, such as a black crystal necklace with faux amber and wear it to a ball instead of your pearl choker. Never wear something you don't really like, no matter how valuable.

Antique Jewellery: What Your Ancestors Knew

It is a common misperception that antique jewellery must be over a hundred years old. For us, antique jewellery consists of beautifully designed and executed pieces made until the 1960s. If you can find it, it will be prohibitively expensive. Today's top jewellers, such as Cartier, Bulgari and Tiffany, target a completely different mass market and taste than in former times. Historically, the top-priced jewellers made their pieces for a sophisticated and demanding elite. Their jewellery was an expression of artistry and craft at the highest level, and the buyer often had a working relationship with the jeweller, who interpreted the client's desires by creating something personal and original. Contemporary jewellery is not modern in quite the same way that Cartier jewellery was modern in the 1920s, when designers were inspired by art, music and theatre. Today's pieces, for the most part, are derivative and profit-driven, produced by designers who must sacrifice their creative integrity by making expensive repetitive baubles for an uninitiated public with money to burn. This market is dominated by diamonds, white of all grades and coloured, natural or enhanced, which find their way into tennis bracelets, ear studs, solitaires, pendants, eternity rings and highly encrusted mega-watches. They are easy to find and undemanding to wear, as long as you have the money to pay for them.

But antique jewellery can be a double-edged sword. As with everything, so much depends on how you wear it. If you put an amber or ivory necklace with white linen cropped trousers and a peach cashmere sweater, it will be cheeky and smart. The same necklace with a flowing paisley caftan is a droopy cliché, unless you are Virginia Woolf. Wear coral and turquoise in the evening; fabulous examples from the greatest jewellers were made during the 1940s. Wear Georgian paste mounted in gold; try garnets, onyx, enamel, citrines, aquamarines, topaz, jet and rock crystal. Look out for a long pair of carved ivory earrings or Indian bone bracelets.

There is a learning process to wearing period jewellery. Your eye becomes educated to wearing brooches, necklaces, clips and bracelets in a new way, with a different aesthetic. Pieces that were fashionable once say something quite unique now and make a comment about past times as well as today's. Practice in front of the mirror, mixing styles and seeing if the effect is pleasing. You can combine period styles with care, but ensure the metals conform in colour. Vary positions and do not aim for the lapel every time. Minimalist trouser suits look stunning with 1940s 'rose-gold' bracelets and earrings because they lend a bit of glamour. Casual clothes look great with Victorian and Edwardian silver. But no matter what you own, do not wear it all at once. Discipline yourself and always take something off before you go out. "Less is more" applies to everything. Be more aware of what you like on yourself. If you are comfortable in those big earrings and a super-sized strand of white South Sea pearls, then by all means wear them. They will always flatter. Ours is the alternative view.

Finally, for those looking for the quality and personal experience we associate with jewellery of yesteryear, there are modern jewellers today who can be commissioned and who have a singular vision: Solange Azagury-Partridge, Elizabeth Gage, James de Givenchy for Taffin, JAR, Kiki McDonough, Judith Ripka, Stephen Webster, Stephen Dweck, Leo de Vroomen and Andrew Grima (still as inventive as he was in the 1960s), to name a few. They are all stylish jewellers whose use of precious and semiprecious stones and new techniques combine to make contemporary and wearable pieces.

To Bead or not to Bead

It is fashionable today to wear beaded bracelets and big intricate chokers that have an aged look about them. They are pretty, can be very decorative, and often look great on young women. But unless they are truly extraordinary in design and made well, they tend to have limited shelf-life. Be careful when you buy these modern confections of metal, glass beads, feathers and hanging leather strips. It might suit you for a night out, but we find you can get bored with this look very fast, and thus the purchase becomes an expensive one-off decision. There are a few costume jewellery designers who can create pieces with lasting power, but we advise that you save your money for something substantial from the past. Antiques were designed with quality in mind, and quality lasts.

Endless Variety

From the vast cornucopia of antique and twentieth-century jewellery, you will have fun deciding which adornments suit you best, and this may alter as time passes and fashions change. In the 1980s, when Ralph Lauren first did his famous Prairie Look, everyone wanted a beautiful cameo to wear at the neck of a tucked lace-and-batiste shirt. Cameos later looked more than a bit passé when the vogue for Calvin Klein minimalism grasped the imagination of smart-looking women. Today's more detailed and decorated look again summons up the desire for an elegant cameo, but always be aware of the need for proper proportion. When it comes to cameos, bigger is better.

The Victorians and Edwardians made rings, lockets, watches and fobs, tiaras, hair ornaments, buttons, belt buckles, seals and chains, collars, chokers as well as rings, earrings, bracelets, brooches and necklaces. They also produced jewelled reticules, tiny mesh handbags, lorgnettes and scarf rings. Remember to keep looking for new trends in old things. We are sure that lockets will be the next big thing.

Affordable Choices

Many women have had a desire for a beautiful cross or heart pendant, but what was once a religious or sentimental motif is now a major fashion statement. The Georgians and Victorians did them first, so why spend thousands on a new, mass-produced diamond cross when, with a little searching at specialist dealers, you can find an antique one that is good value and features unmatchable craftsmanship? Your friends will be pea-green with envy, and isn't that what it is all about? If you want to be sweet, share your source – with luck, a reliable dealer – but your pals will never find exactly the same thing.

Get to know the dealers. They have a passion for collecting their "art works" and will share their knowledge and commitment to quality with their steady customers. If they get to know your taste, they will contact you when they find something special, and not necessarily in a pushy way. A good dealer will buy what he or she likes, so if you have changed your mind, there is always the possibility that they will take the piece back. They take responsibility for their jewels, will repair them, and if you tire of your little treasure, they will usually exchange or sell it for you. They can be friends indeed.

Anti-Conformism

In choosing to explore the world of antique jewellery, you have just learned another way of showing your independence as a thinker and self-stylist. You have logged into history and romance. You have separated yourself from the madding crowd. You are a patron of the arts, a collector. You are recycling in the very best sense. You are taking from the past and imbuing it with new and relevant meaning. You are showing high standards and values to others and keeping alive a history. This is special in a way that a nice big rock can never be.

CHAPTER ELEVEN

Scents and Nonsense

Blending memory, eroticism, femininity and the intellect in a heady mix, perfume is one of life's more enjoyable complexities. Your first experience of perfume was probably your mother's. She may have worn Joy, Sortilege or Chanel No. 5, incredibly heady and floral scents with a powdery, female sophistication. We will always associate them with fur coats, tiny purple violets in a corsage, cocktail dresses, hats and glamour. As young girls, we might have been given bottles of Yardley or White Lilac, light and lyrical fragrances suitable, our mothers thought, for young girls. Naturally, as time went on, we began to think differently.

For many of us growing up, perfume became a must – part of the arsenal of seduction. We've all been through some dubious stages, wearing the strongest-smelling brands that reeked for miles around. A favourite at seventeen might have been Jungle Gardenia by Fabergé. And who could forget Dior's Poison at thirty-five? Most of today's new fragrances are equally potent and unavoidable. They can be vulgar and aggressive, and they last and last. They are so enduring that they can be difficult to remove from your clothes or even furniture. Motivated by making immediate profits from an unwitting public rather than creating a multidimensional classic, manufacturers today use the most powerful, longest-lasting oils and chemical ingredients for maximum, instant impact.

A perfume launch is like promoting an action-packed movie production. It costs the earth, depends on a young audience, opens everywhere and dies within a month or two. Today, every fashion house has a perfume, merely a part of a diverse financial portfolio every company seeks. Most disappear. There are, however, two modern perfumes that have a genuine quality to them: those of Michael Kors and Carolina Herrera. They are original, feminine and smell gorgeously of white flowers. Thankfully, most of us have outgrown the need to announce ourselves with perfume before we've even walked into a room.

Perfume is all about "notes," layers that unfold as you wear it, a personality that reveals itself through the day and evening. Perfume is about *sex*. Not the rutting, grunting stuff we have shoved at us all the time, but the essence of what is feminine. We must approach this subject with some caution because everyone responds differently to olfactory experiences, so many of which are steeped in memory (think Proust).

Real perfume will always and forever be French, the foundation of every French woman's idea about herself. It can be rich and mysterious, floral and innocent, lyrical and virginal, or sophisticated and sharp. It says reams about personality. It evokes idiosyncrasies, strength and always does so in the most personal way, up close. For women of a certain age, sophisticated perfume is a necessity, not a choice. We may no longer be able to come across as freshly scrubbed linen or a newly mown lawn. We are not a peach-and-parsley salad. We are not a cup of cappuccino with a dusting of mocha. We are not aftershave; sandalwood is too masculine for us. We need Bulgarian rose and tuberose. We are hyacinth and Chinese camellia. You cannot smell our perfume ten seats away in a restaurant. You have to sit right down next to us and whisper in our ears before you get the full impact.

When we talk about perfume, we are talking Mozart, Bach, Cole Porter and jazz – eternal classics. We are modern and sceptical and wear Chanel No. 22. When feeling sporty, we spray on L'Air du Temps or Calèche. When we seduce, we wear Mille by Patou, Jolie Madame or Fracas. We search out the old marques – Guerlain and Creed.

Small perfumeries such as Les Scenteurs in London and Barney's (downstairs) in New York feature row upon delicious row of the best of the best. Many are unexploited classics, and some are newer varieties, such as Serge Lutens. Your visits will be met with an understanding, passion-driven staff who will guide you through the intricacies of the art. We adore old-fashioned bottles of Arpège, Robert Piguet's Bandit, Annick Goutal's Ce Soir ou Jamais, Passion and Violet. We love Caron's Tabac Blond, En Avion, Fleur de Rocailles and Lancôme's Magie. We will not wear anything called Cool, Maybe Baby, Traction, Obsession, Ooze, Rush, Addiction, Therapy and Hallucinogen. We do not want to be hit directly in the olfactories with the equivalent of a Mickey Finn.

We want rapture and *je ne sais quoi*. We want a twinge of sharp green to wake us in the morning, a touch of spice to tweak the nervous system and a deep, dark sense of magic, always. We want the originals because they have not yet been equalled. We want to reach back into our being and remember that we are still the same person, only older.

It's worth noting that there are some new small perfumeurs out there. One new favourite is Bois Blond by Parfumerie Generale in Paris, but the staying power is questionable, both in terms of skin and economics. Small brands are bought up by large companies, and then the mass marketing begins and the individuality and creativity are often lost.

CHAPTER TWELVE

Scarves and
How They Work

Walking down the streets of Paris, we marvel at the twists and turns of Parisian women's scarves. Made of silk, wool, chiffon, challis, leather, fur and cashmere, they appear tied on the neck, hanging on one shoulder, draped across the shoulders and back, around the waist, as a halter-necked top, looped onto handbags, folded to fit through belt loops, fluttering from the wrist and draped around the hips like a novel mini-skirt. A French woman's use of her scarf is full of pizzazz. In addition to its utility, the scarf is the signifier of style.

Utility comes first. For this reason, scarves come in many different shapes and sizes, from the smallest handkerchief to the grandest double-sized pashmina or stole. A scarf keeps your neck and shoulders warm. Wrapped over your head, it keeps you cosy and dry and protects your coiffed hair from the elements. It holds up your jeans when used as a sash. It saves clothing from body oils. Tucked in, it helps preserve the necklines of sweaters, coats, furs and jackets.

But it is so much more than utilitarian. The scarf is the ultimate finishing touch, like a man's tie, and can be used similarly to add a flash of colour to an otherwise dull outfit. It can be a substitute for jewellery, or the background for a wonderful brooch. The scarf can emit a number of messages to the beholder, and silk will always be *the* status symbol and indicator of good taste.

Let us start at the top: the basic Hermès scarf, the quintessence of head and neck fashion. Hermès scarves are unique, and you cannot have

enough of them. Women collect them like jewels. Aside fror
out a powerful status message, they are softly luxurious, h
designs and sophisticated colours. They are seasonal, in tł
four; they are seasonal, in that they can be continually ren
are witty, artistic, classic, literate and can be worn with anyu....
heavy silk prints whisper class. They can be attached to a belt buckle,
draped into a summer basket as a lining or tied around your belongings
for safe-keeping. They can function like a man's tie, or turban, depending on your mood. They can be used as a sling in an emergency – in
other words, this small and rather uncomplicated piece of material can
express good taste, even on a broken arm. And all this for under £200.

That is the power of association. What is a Hermès scarf but a bril-
liantly conceived, walking advertisement for a company that mainly specializes in the finest, handmade leather goods in the world. When you
wear a Hermès scarf, you are saying "I know what is good, what is chic,
timeless, worth having, buying, stealing, borrowing and inheriting." You
would never throw away a Hermès scarf, no more than one of their
handbags. In this world of ephemera and overexposure, there is still a
mystique to this marque.

The chiffon scarf does not need a brand name on it because it is
about romance, lyricism and self-expression. It is simply about drifts of
colour, imagination and texture. It ties like a bow, or mists around your
neck. It drapes over your bare shoulders, concealing and revealing. It
looks chic bundled and tied around your neck with a suit. It covers and
flirts over an evening gown. The chiffon scarf disguises flaws in the neck,
draws attention to the eyes and functions like makeup, bringing light to
the face. It can be funky and shredded-looking, wispy, modern, patterned or plain. Even in leopard print, it does not look tarty. Always tie it
loosely: it is not a bandage so keep it flowing.

Long or triangular scarves made of cashmere, wool, or silk and wool
combined fall loosely under the current appellation of pashmina. Strictly
speaking, the recent pashmina phenomenon is the reworking of a classic
piece of apparel known as the stole. In the 1980s custom officials and animal rights campaigners noticed that rich women were buying something
called the *shatoosh*. These were woven in India and Nepal from the finest
and lightest of cashmeres, and in such alarming numbers that the little
fleecy goats from which they were taken were literally freezing to death
after being shorn. Even the hardest of fashionista hearts took the animals'
plight seriously, and could no longer buy into the fable that this softest of
hairs was being simply gathered off bushes in the high Himalayas. The
highly desirable *shatoosh* became politically incorrect.

In its place, however, an idea was born: the politically correct pash-

...na. This item, which has passed into the realm of commonplace, is now available in every grade, size, material and colour. It can be embroidered, tie-dyed, set with sequins and stones, embellished with lace, fringed with leather or beads or lined with fur. Fashion writers deride its ubiquity and dismiss it as a chic statement, but it still appears in every shop, under every label and on every street corner because its utility goes beyond fashion. It is warm, its colours flatter, and it has a feminine softness next to the skin.

The more luxurious and softer cloths take the colours best, and last the longest. Cheap brands tend to pill, thin out, wrinkle and lose their feel and lustre. As we live in such a variable climate, the pashmina is a must. It can be folded up into the neatest little square and popped into your handbag if the chill winds blow away, and is just about the only accessory we can buy to complement a gorgeous new outfit without competing with it. In a highly embellished version, it can take you to any special event. Everybody makes them. At the top end, Loro Piana's versions are unbeatable for their softness; for those on a tighter budget, try Pickett, which makes imaginative and pretty examples.

CHAPTER THIRTEEN

Bags

These days, handbags are the biggest sellers in every shop. No one seems to be buying anything much in the way of clothes. Young, middle-aged and old alike are spending their entire budget on this single piece. Why? Part of the answer lies in the fact that clothing lines are just too disappointing – our mantra throughout this entire book. We are in a state of clothes overload. The industry has realized this and is forcing accessories down our collective throats. They know we cannot resist them because we need them. If you cannot find a delicious top or skirt, try a handbag Madam.

In spite of the mania, however, the handbag is a powerful expression of who you are and how you feel about yourself. A scuffed, shapeless, worn-out bag may say the same about you. Your handbag should reflect your personal style and fulfil your practical needs.

The very retro Hermès Kelly or Birkin bags have been the most desirable of recent years. There are unlimited copies and versions (Pickett makes excellent reproductions at a tenth of the price). Martha Stewart made the fashion faux pas of appearing in court with her very expensive Birkin bag. An observant editor spotted it and condemned her for her elitism and arrogance. It might have been in good taste but an appalling choice, given her indictment for insider trading. It showed little social conscience and by carrying it she seemed to be saying, "I am rich, successful, proud of it, I am who I am, take it or leave it." She should have accessorized her correctly conservative suit with a small black clutch bag, unmarked by a logo, and carried her notebooks and other paraphernalia in a black nylon carry-all. Expensive good taste is a bad idea for the courtroom.

There is a huge amount of choice in handbags and every designer is making them, so here are a few rules when buying one.

Always buy the best quality you can afford. Years ago, Diana Vreeland pointed out that you could get away with wearing a cheap dress as long as you had expensive shoes and a bag to accessorize it. Clearly, you will need at least two bags, one for the day and one for the evening. You will need two colours, black and brown. What about size? Should a small woman wear a very big handbag? Yes, when it is beautiful, chic and fun. The bigger the handbag in a great colour (try purple or wine red), the better the look, but try to avoid resembling a porter. Bowling-ball bags are also awkward, being an impractical shape and bulky (even if you are only carrying your house keys). Should a big woman wear a small handbag? Yes, when it is made of precious skin or intricately woven. It may be slightly retro, in which case it can hang off her gloved wrist. Anyone can carry a clutch tucked under their arm. We all crate around far too much anyway, and a small bag will restrict you in a healthy way. You will avoid being weighed down with too much stuff; take the essentials and leave it at that. (But if you feel guilty because you missed your weight-lifting session at the gym, feel free to carry a bit more.)

The shoulder-strap issue: some physiotherapists say that you should never wear bags with shoulder straps because they pull at your neck and shoulders, unbalance your body and cause untold damage. However, the shoulder strap is the hands-free choice, and thus we cannot condemn it. We recommend wearing a small one across your chest, like a bandolier, for comfort and security; this is almost mugger repellent. Your posture will improve as well as your look. Shoulder bags look young and sexy, and there is even a military aspect about them, which can add a bit of sexual ambiguity.

Avoid blatant logos, although these days this is easier said than done. We live in a label-crazed society, but why should you feel compelled to adorn yourself with huge designer initials, motifs, names? Look for bags with a minimum of metal tags, buckles, hooks, strands and fussy appendages. Leave the logos to the teenagers and wannabes. More than maddening is the arrival of cheap copies and fakes, many of which are virtually indistinguishable from the real thing. These are usually covered in logos, so logo-less models will only heighten your profile and differentiate you from the hoi polloi. The only exception is the label that no one recognizes – not even you. This is a unique find, and you can flaunt it as you wish.

Although we love a good circus when it comes to town, the current vogue for expensive, glitzy, over-manipulated, brightly coloured, metal-adorned handbags does no one any favours. What is the point? Again, this is rock 'n' roll for the young, and cheap copies can be bought on beaches from Asia to America. Leave it to them, this is not a good style for us.

Other recommendations: Bottega Veneta's recent lines of woven bags are stunning and innovative, available in subtle or radiant colours but steeply priced. What was once a semi-affordable brand has now gone to the luxury end of the market. They make excellent bags – lightweight, comfortable to carry, well-sized, classic and chic. If you can find the money for one, start by dispensing with your chiropractor because your poor back will be so much better thanks to Bottega's clever engineering.

Pickett does quality versions of classic styles. Furla is great in the middle range and sells matching gloves, key holders, wallets and shoes. Anya Hindmarch does some creative things with prints. Mulberry is classic English and cannot be faulted, with a many-buckled twist these days. Luella Bartley, much loved by models, is a name to look out for. We like Longchamps for its utility and style, with bags available in leather, canvas and nylon, in all sizes, shapes and colours. They are a French woman's must for a discreet, logo-less elegance. Visit Etro for their distinctly patterned paisley bags and carry-alls. Tanner Krolle is young and trendy, and their pieces are remarkably well made. Loro Piana is a luxury cashmere manufacturer and clothier, but they also make attractive handbags of the highest-quality skins, which are hand-finished, less expensive than Hermès (but perhaps more expensive than they should be) and made in limited numbers for a discreet and wealthy clientele.

If you happen to find yourself in the duty-free section of Milan's airport, there is a shop called Bric's that makes wonderful bags and luggage. Airports are a good source for bags as you may well stumble across models you have not seen in town, at discounted prices. Department stores are also good sources for non-branded bags.

Bags for the Evening
This is a complicated subject because so much depends on what outfits you have for the evening. If you own mainly black dresses and suits, then your choice of bag is virtually limitless because you can add sparkle and colour as you wish. However, if a glance at your formal clothes indicates that you own a rather disparate collection of multicoloured pieces, each strikingly different from the other, then you need an evening bag that is neutral and goes with the lot. Perhaps two bags.

Megan Park has created lovely little embroidered and beaded 'shoppers' for evenings. Gone are the days when we could just run out with a bag containing a red lipstick and latchkey. We need our glasses and cell phone. Lulu Guinness has invented quirky bags that would suit your granddaughter as well as you. They are witty, useful and fun – big enough to hold the essentials and not desperately expensive. Judith Leiber has produced the world's most recognized evening bags, in silk, retro 'granny' styles or in bejewelled novelty shapes that are moulded into animals, fruits, vegetables and minerals. Although much pho-tographed in the magazines and subscribed to by a coterie of devoted fans, we find her bags a bit ostentatious and expensive beyond their worth. They make a big statement. If you should ever drop one, the crys-tals fall off and fly everywhere. If you already own one, wear it with a very plain dark suit, and it could look chic.

Old crocodile can still be found in the antique markets, along with a huge selection of embroidered bags. Some of these are stunning and show a care and attention to detail that you seldom come across today. These one-off pieces might have beads, tassels, or be encrusted with paste jewels, mounted with faux ivory and amber, gilt metal or bakelite handles, and come in fabrics such as crushed velvet, satin, needlepoint, silk and metallic materials. They are frequently good value. If you do not trust your own judgment in the markets, try the following who sell wonderfully evocative vintage and antique-inspired bags. In London, visit Angela Hale, off Bond Street; Butler & Wilson on South Molton Street; and Basia Zarzy-cka at Sloane Square. (Warning: use these bags when you wear a sharp, minimal evening suit, not as part of a 1960s 'love-in' look or you risk look-ing like you are off to a fancy dress party.) Look in Gina for sparkle.

Care

You may be a tidy lady who has stored all her great handbags in covers, for years. But if you are not, you should start now. Every time you buy a good handbag, treat it like a piece of art. Store it in the flannel it came in; there is a reason why it is included in the purchase price. Protect it from scratches, and polish it occasionally with leather cream. In the rain, carry a nylon handbag – leave the good one at home – as the finest leather can blister. Heavy-duty nylon bags are almost indestructible, and they look smart.

If you have an older handbag that is damaged but a beloved treasure, do not dream of throwing it out. Take it to a specialist leather workshop (often this doubles as a shoe repairer), where they may be able to re-sew ripped stitches, remove stains and smooth over cracks. If you take the piece back to the shop where you bought it originally, and it is a leading known brand, they should be willing to restore and repair the bag, usual-ly for a fee.

Let Us Be Modern

People look on Ebay for Hermès handbags and other top brands, but be warned, they can be more expensive at auction than in the shops, and there is a good reason for this: you cannot find them in the shops. There are lengthy waiting lists for certain models and a queue of eager purchasers a mile long. On internet shopping sites, however, you may see a large selection because some clever vendors have somehow managed to buy up every bag they can get their hands on from far-flung places across the globe. These sellers have cornered the market for Birkins and Kellys. We do not know how they do it, but it makes for good surfing. Do plenty of research before you buy something on the net, particularly if you are spending, sight unseen, at least £10,000 (yes, you read that correctly) for a black crocodile Birkin described as "never used." Read the user commentaries, and the services they offer. Beware fakes.

You can find other good buys on Ebay. We discovered a 'bucket' handbag for less than £20 with a matching wallet, decorated with two velvet Pekinese dogs. It is adorable, utterly silly and possibly the chicest thing we have seen in ages. You can find many bags that capture the imagination and have fun with them.

CHAPTER FOURTEEN

Belts and Other
Mid-body Experiences

For grown-up women, belts are not a functional thing for holding up your clothes. They are for adornment. They add spice, make your wardrobe more flexible and new, and provide shape and distraction. They add fashion attitude because they can exploit the trend of the moment in an abstract way, without demanding that you do the whole look. They express the idea that you know what is happening in fashion and that you are smart enough to use it to create a personal statement. The belt transcends age and condition.

Anyone can wear a belt if they understand their own body shape. Belts have sex appeal because they have links to bondage. Think constraint and release issues, tension and relaxation, the concept of undressing and slowly unbuckling....You get the picture. Belts on the hipline emphasize several erogenous areas of the body: hips, curves, and derrières. As we age, our mid-sections tend to get a bit broader, and our legs and hips can get slimmer. Between the waist and hips is a good place for a belt.

Belts stay in style because they can be unique in themselves. They may be stored away for what seems like forever, and still trundled out years later to say something different from when you first wore them. Give away belts made of fake skin; they fool no one. It is almost better to wear plastic that says it's plastic – see-through vinyl printed with strawberries, why not? Belts play with textures and shape. Patent leather contrasts well with something soft, like grey flannel. Furry animal prints like zebra or cheetah look good with something silky and smooth. Chains and grommets toughen up something predictable and conservative. It is all about mixing it up, yin and yang.

A Few Belt Rules

Forget about belts that cinch the waist: hour-glass-shaping body belts, corset belts with laces and elasticated five-inch belts. We know fashionistas are enamoured by the Fifties-look flared skirt with the wide belt, but please leave this for your younger sisters who still have their hourglass figures. Avoid too much shiny gold metal and excessive glitzy chains. Gold plate, if not the highest quality, rubs off and starts to look cheap as it ages. Pewter metal is okay, silver is great, blackened metal is chic and right now.

At the risk of sounding repetitive, avoid designer logos if you can. They are obvious, boring and dated. One year's logo is next year's joke. Even still, there are some logos that we cannot avoid easily, such as the Hermes 'H' and the Chanel double 'C'. Everyone seems to want one, and almost everyone seems to have one. But you must ask yourself, "Is this look doing anything for me now? Do I need this label? Am I not a grown up?" If the answer is "this look is not doing me any favours," then put the belt away for another time (or planet). Retain your individuality.

An exception to going logo-less: if you love a certain designer's clothes but do not have the money for an outfit top-to-toe, forget the logo rule and just buy the belt, with all its bells and whistles. At least you will have a cherished accessory from the collection, and you can celebrate the fact that you have chosen, with discretion and restraint, something very "now."

We love the look of a pleated scarf, threaded through a buckle and worn as a belt. Become your own belt maker. Find some beaded ornaments, paste jewellery or antique medallions and pin them onto fabric sashes, leather or suede cords. They will look excellent with jeans and break up the inevitable tedium of the black skirt or trousers. Designers such as Marni and Prada have been producing these eccentric pieces for the last few years, but you can probably make better ones yourself for a tenth of the price.

Belts are transformative. They are jewels. Belts make black, grey, navy and beige look interesting. The art of belt dressing is very often the juxtaposition of the classic with the somewhat incongruous – the witty, daring, high fashion or idiosyncratic. But if you choose to feature a great belt, then be sure that is the ONE thing that you accessorize with; dispense with all other adornments (wedding rings and watches are okay) or you might look like a Christmas tree. Worse, if you load on every detail from a designer's collection – the shoes, bag, belt, charm bracelet, earrings – you will end up functioning as a promotional catalogue. Think laterally with your belt; practice combinations in front of a mirror as you would if you were pinning on a brooch. Try it higher or lower, with different colours and fabrics. Love its flexibility and feminine qualities. Relish it because it is your chance to express those little quirks in your personality.

Where do we find belts that are highly original and not blazoned with advertising? There is no set answer, but start your search in some of the antique markets and smaller out-of-the-way craftshops and boutiques. There are excellent shops in Paris, such as those on the Rue Cherche Midi; in London, try Camden Passage, Alfie's antique market, Greys antique market and shops such as Agatha, Musa, Butler & Wilson, Paul and Joe, and branches of Accessorize and East on the high street. Gabriella Ligenza, on Ellis Street in Chelsea, has a unique collection of hats, jewellery and belts that you will find no where else. Belgian designer Anne Demeulemeester specializes in leather and suede belts (no logo), which are introduced with each season's clothes. They become an integral part of her outfits, always innovative and can be used for years to adapt to any other ensemble. They are the rock face of fashion.

Every time you are in a foreign city, look for accessories in local markets. Use your imagination. If you are very conservative but want a neat, original and unflamboyant look, twist some fake pearls around a black velvet ribbon, tie them slightly below the waist and knot. This is especially attractive on women who still have a waist, even if they are larger than a size 10. If you do not have one any more, best to keep the scarves at neck level. For evening, with black silk trousers or a slim-line black wool skirt and sweater, try wrapping a suede or velvet oblong scarf with a fringe around the upper hips. Secure this with a big, fake, bejewelled brooch. Wear boots and a dashing black cashmere scarf.

Beautiful and classic belts come in crocodile, ostrich, kidskin, lizard, suede – in every colour, but not white. We do not like white belts on mature women, except maybe in the dead heat of summer, made out of plaited leather and worn with a matching pair of flat sandals. Otherwise, there is practically nothing on earth that looks good with a white belt, unless you are a physiotherapist or work in a sanitarium.

CHAPTER FIFTEEN

Shoes, Beautiful Shoes

L et us go then, you and I, to talk of shoes. They have an importance in this world that cannot be emphasized enough. Talk
about foot fetishes, every woman (and some men) have one.
Open her cupboard, and you will find a psychologically driven,
Aladdin's cave of shoes. Shoes represent hours of tortuous search, of
completely emotional hits and runs. There will be favourites that will
never be tossed out, shoes for wearing only in the rain, shoes we save for
special dresses or occasions, shoes that hurt and shoes that don't. Shoes
can represent devotion to an ideal configuration of the foot, or they can
act as a kind of promiscuity that satisfies for a fleeting, ecstatic moment.
They are an expression of our many-sided natures in a way that clothes
can never be. Form can follow function, and function can follow form,
but the shoe is a statement in itself as to how we feel about ourselves and
where our vulnerabilities lie.

Pass any shoe store, especially a favourite, and you will recognize the
feeling of welling desire. It might be a tantalizing high heel in peach
python with a bow in the back that has stopped you in your tracks. Not
very useful, but *oh my*. We might be drooling over black, sponged-soled
Hogan sports shoes. They murmur seductively to us, not just because
they look comfortable or active, but because they say: "I am your
younger self. I am the girl who runs down the street with a streaming
flag of Timotei-washed hair." Yet another pair of shoes might speak, in
an authoritative tone: "I am comfortable, but I am not an old fuddy-
duddy – I am of the moment."

Shoes can express an entire range of attitudes and emotions. They are a long-term investment to spice up boring old suits. They are a short-term fix to uplift your spirits to a Stepford Wives moment in an otherwise very challenging day. They symbolize life itself in some sense. Where would we be without our feet, our transportation, our "places to go, people to see" kind of life? If you are feeling low, you might think that a new outfit would cheer you up. It won't, but try a new pair of shoes. So much more affordable, and you can throw away today's supply of St. John's Wort.

Thank goodness the fashion industry thrives on our need for shoes. Designers who fail to produce anything of value for us are still making money from accessories, and they have found a suitable outlet for their need to innovate. Lucky us, we can wear them all – last year's stilettos, this year's wedges, another year's flatties. Low heels, high heels, no heels – all have a utilitarian and an illuminating contribution to make.

Low Life

Low heels are for the very tall, the very active, the very sporty, the youthful, ladies who like to walk a lot and ladies with shorter husbands – in other words, the no-nonsense you. Flat sandals and mules look the most chic in summer with cropped trousers or shorter skirts. Trainers, lace-up Oxfords, loafers and flats can be elegant, comfortable, relaxed and can bring a dressy suit down to a more accessible level during the day. If you have a long foot, however, do be careful of those wonderful man-tailored brogues, such as those made by Fratelli Rossetti. Unless you like the look of a canal boat or are showing a new interest in cross-dressing, stick to more feminine versions. If you have tiny little tootsies, those same brogues could have a gender playfulness that ask "Does she, or doesn't she?" Do try to avoid the Miss Marple look, however. Tod's are the ultimate player in this low-down game (and how we love the games they play). Their delicious loafers and moccasins in chartreuse or tomato-red are to die for.

And God Created High Heels

*Ah....*Manolo Blahnik, Christian Louboutin, Sergio Rossi, Jimmy Choo, Prada, Miu Miu, Chanel, Gucci, Dolce & Gabbana, Gina – they are a few of the best, if the most widely known. These designers provide the daintiest, most erotically charged shoes anywhere. Just watch women trying on the latest sexy shoes, with their eyes glazed as they wait expectantly, hoping against hope that this wonderful, evocative item comes in their size (and that their credit cards can manage the extra burden). Oh joy, when the box arrives. Oh happiness, when they fit. Oh misery, when they hurt (but you are going to have them anyway). We may be prejudiced, but high heels are the kind of medicine that every woman needs. Admittedly, they cannot accompany you through the wild landscapes or on a bicycle trip across Normandy's landing beaches. And you may have foot and balance problems that preclude the tallest models. But a beautiful pair of toffee-coloured, lizard, high-heeled sling-backs gives you confidence that no amount of comfort can. Just try a pair of stilettos and look at your legs. They are artfully stretched, and the arch looks higher. You start walking the walk, and talking the talk. You feel cool. You feel tall. You feel lean and mean.

The key to this look is finding the right last and heel height. You might have a bunion or two, be suffering from an occasional corn or callous or an ingrown toe-nail. Remember: chiropody first, shoes later. Assuming that your feet are still useable, follow these rules:

Try new shoes on in the morning, then return to the shop later in the day and try them again. Time consuming, yes, but our feet change with the climate and even over the course of several hours. So for the best fit, two tries will usually do it.

Be very demanding. Do not apologize. If something hurts (say, at the throat of the shoe, on the point of a toe, or at the heel), reject it immediately, no matter how much you love it. No amount of pressure from a sales assistant should make you buy shoes that are uncomfortable or unsuitable in any way.

If you have small feet and ankles, ankle straps can be sexy and cute. If your feet are larger and your ankles less than chicken-bone frail, ankle straps will cut the length of your leg and thicken it up. The only exception is a flesh-coloured shoe that blends in with your skin and stocking tones. A little jewelled buckle would be flirtatious.

A word to the wise: crocodile shoes are gorgeous, cost the earth, are stiff as boards no matter how much you pay and rot as soon as they hit wet pavement. Unless you have money to burn and feet as flexible as rubber tubing, do not bother buying them. Otherwise you will find yourself crying wildly when both you and your destroyed crocs are soaked through in a deluge. Lizard and snakeskin are more pliable and cheaper. If you must have the look of croc, buy fake.

Toe Shapes

Toe shapes vary from season to season, and pointy ones have been with us since the Middle Ages. They flatter most women (if it is the right last) because they elongate feet and make them appear narrow and elegant. Round toes might be more comfortable but can look a bit clumsy. For fun, think Minnie Mouse shoes, revived by Marni and other designers for all seasons. Square toes are a legacy of Oliver Cromwell's days and are going out of date. If you buy square-toed shoes, look for a sense of whimsy. Try zebra-skinned prints, or grey or white lizard.

Your elegant new heels will rule your life and change the way you think, walk, sit and cross your legs. Like Moira Shearer's red shoes, they will make you dance and dance (without having to throw yourself off a balcony). You will reach into your cupboard and bring them out to make your frumpiest suit seem new. You will flex your ankles, show your knees and enjoy the process of living so much more.

These Boots are Made for Walking

Why do we wear and love boots? Is it the memory of Emma Peel in *The Avengers*, in her kinky, up-to-the-thigh, black patent-leather ones? Or is it because they disguise flaws, keep rain off our legs, keep us warm, and enable us to wear socks in winter and give us support? Is it because they are young and sexy? Here is the dichotomy – utility versus beauty.

Boots come in every height, colour, fabric and shape. Why are fashionable boots better? A good pair will always make you feel feminine, even sexy. Perhaps it is the military connection, or something to do with whips? We all love a uniform. Maybe there's an association with Puss 'n' Boots, the ultimate cat woman? Is it that "principal boy" thing? Whichever fantasy comes to mind, their enduring popularity speaks volumes: soft leather or suede rising up the calf is sensual, flattering and mysterious. Let your audience imagine what lies beyond.

When we wear boots, we do not have to bother with the reality of our calves and ankles. Some of us do not like these parts, which may be a little thicker or skinnier than we would wish; the ankle may be a bit too robust, without that lovely curve inward. Lacrosse and ballet lessons may have knotted your muscles and made them bulge slightly. A beautiful boot disguises and enhances.

Ankle boots are good for the ego. If you have shapely calves, slim ankles and are long from knee to foot, this look says, "Notice me." Our mothers wore them as rain or snow boots, but today's models are far from that kind of innocent utility. Even if your legs are less than perfect, you could wear a pair of black, stiletto-heeled ankle boots with black opaque hose and give the world a lesson in strutting. There is a real feminine supercharge in this kind of footgear. With pencil skirts, they are so chic. Under trousers, they keep the illusion of the long, slim leg underneath. Evening versions come in suede, velvet, brocade or satin with tiny diamante buckles. We love the look of a long brown lacy skirt with a cashmere top and a pair of bronze satin evening boots. Try a leopard pair from Walter Steiger. Add a little fur boa, and have fun.

BODY
PARTS

CHAPTER SIXTEEN

The Little and Large
Conundrum

W omen come in all shapes and sizes. There are women with muscular, rangy bodies who might have played rugby forwards at university, and there are little bird-like creatures who remain essentially boy-girls all their lives. Some of us are truly rolypoly, and no matter how much we diet there will always be a soft roundness to our bodies. Short of body resculpturing, round people are round. Square women are square, teensies are tiny, and wiry athletic types are out on the golf course in culottes, not concerned in the slightest.

Disproportionates
We all respond differently to the impossibly beautiful, air-brushed "model girl" standard. As we get older and presumably wiser, we know we cannot achieve *that* – nor should we want to at this stage. With the exception of the lucky few, many of us always were or are now disproportionate in our shape. We have spread or atrophied, we have grown bosoms or lost them. Our hips have dropped or widened, even if in the first flush of maidenhood we always were bottom- or top-heavy. These changes can be an advantage or disadvantage, depending on your point of view.

A woman with a long slim waist, high bosom and narrow shoulders but wider hips and thighs can easily disguise the disharmony between the upper and lower halves. She can wear A-line dresses or long, swingy skirts and punctuate her waist with a belt. She looks slim and youthful with polo-necks, tucked in sweaters and nipped-in, waisted jackets. She's attractive in cargo pants (if cleverly cut and not too low in the waist) and flowing, palazzo shapes. Very tailored skirts and pleated trousers will minimize her hips and direct the eye upwards. She looks best in triangular shapes with small fur collars or long coats with tied belts.

Her slim-legged, tiny-ankled, no-bottom sister with the big bosom and thickened waist can play different tricks. This can be a difficult body type to dress. Her stock in trade is trousers: flat-fronted, narrow-legged, with strictly tailored, slightly long jacket shapes on top. She neutralizes her thickened middle and concentrates on the contrasts of top and bottom. She uses her bosom, neck and broader shoulders as a focus and concentrates on necklines, big chunky necklaces and trim boots or slim shoes to show off the extremes of chest and ankles. She can wear fitted sweaters but must be aware of the inevitable 'roll' effect at the sides. This should be disguised with a 'shirt' jacket, scarf or cape. If she wears skirts, they should be knee-length or slightly above, to concentrate attention on her legs. She, lucky lady, can wear sexy ankle boots, multicoloured, lace-up or even flat shoes, to make the most of her body and leg type. She can play with broad-shouldered looks, big fur collars, bunched-up scarves and hats.

Large Ladies

Calling all size-16 ladies! You are often referred to as "outsizes," but this is unfair as the whole world is getting bigger – it has something to do with protein. The problem is finding clothes in the length and breadth that you need. There are brands like Marina Rinaldi, and it does a good job of translating style to those women who cannot chop off their bodies. If you are not much over size 16, trouser lengths from regular manufacturers, such as Max Mara, are longer than the average (most women have to shorten everything). The real problem is proportion. When designers create a piece, they have an "ideal" body type in mind, and ladies over five feet ten inches and ten stone are *not it.* That said, you can find manufacturers that deal with your "build": Louise Kennedy, Daks, Aquascutum, Emporio Armani, Paddy Campbell, Caroline Charles, Eskander, Ghost, Issey Miyake and Nicole Farhi are a few. It is a matter of searching diligently. Larger ladies can wear immense handbags, flowing caftans, big furry coats, high boots, big prints, pancake-sized or long drop earrings and monumental Byzantine-style necklaces. They can swan down the street in huge capes and look imposing and desirable at the same time. How we admire the tall, rangy woman with her look of natural authority.

Smaller Sister

You might think that being small, or what the manufacturers call "petite," is no problem at all. Every one of us must have had a cute, doll-like friend smaller than five feet two inches who all the fellows craved. She was a pocket Venus, so adorable, a little figurine to hang off a big, strong man – arm candy, human jewellery. How we envied her miniature body perfection when we were younger. The trouble is, we all grew up, and those tiny little creatures started widening or shrinking or both. What was once fragile and feminine can develop into something nearly invisible over time. Furthermore, it is nearly impossible to find sizes. You might well ask how this can be when manufacturers such as Prada specialize in the underweight and undersized (even for tinies, a rib removal may be required to get the zipper up). When you are five feet two, eyes of blue, and have a frame like a mosquito, your size starts at 34 in France, 36 to 38 in the rest of Europe and 000 (yes, triple zero) to 2 in the United States. These very small sizes tend to sell out fast. Everything is on a smaller scale – shoulders, bust, hips, leg lengths – and you will be overwhelmed if you try to carry a luggage-sized handbag, no matter how smart it looks. You cannot wear broad-brimmed hats (unless you are Anoushka Hempel, who made them a speciality). You must not drown yourself in long-haired furs. Fortunately, at the less expensive end of fashion, there are cheaper brands cut smaller to save money on fabric, and you have far more economic opportunities than your larger sisters. Zara, Top Shop, Jigsaw, Karen Millen, L.K. Bennett, Marc (of Marc Jacobs) and Gap tend to start at smaller sizes. At the high end, Chanel, Azzedine Alaïa, Miu Miu, Paul Smith, Rick Owens and Proenza Schouler all love the littler ladies.

Small women look best when wearing fitted, tailored clothing. Forget smock tops and baggy trousers; Puffa jackets, chunky belts and thigh-high boots are best left to the taller. Look for structure and definition, you do not want to be swamped in layers. You can elongate yourself with solid colours, shorter jackets, pencil skirts, tapered trousers and high heels. If anything flaps or moves violently on your body, reject it.

There are two problems to note. Little ladies can have large bosoms that weigh them down and cause great dressing problems. Short of surgery, they must deal with the difficulties of sizing on top (see "Disproportionates," above) with the added challenge of their height. Minimizing bras can help, and undergarments like Spanx will eliminate bumps and lumps even on the unusually petite. In addition, short women should not feel obliged to wear the highest platform heels. It is not easy to teeter about in those 5-inch dillies. Be comfortable and accept your shorter stature. If you must walk tall, wear a wedge heel for better balance. Try a kitten heel for a change, or even venture out in flatties. Remember: your ultra-feminine appeal was once based on being tiny. You still have it.

Body Dysmorphia

There are some women who suffer from a condition, loosely and medically identified as body dysmorphia: the excessive concern about a particular aspect of their body. Some are obsessively insecure about their bosoms, their chins, noses, hair and the very length of their arms or legs. At the teenage level, this can evolve into anorexia. The anorexic who is starving emotionally and physically sees herself in a distorted way. No matter how thin she is, she is always too fat. She is eating up her own body as she is torn apart by her own imagined inadequacies and by society's dictates. Even children of five or six, in these late capitalist times, are influenced by models, magazines, media imagery, movies and the running commentaries of their peers about being too fat. Thin- and weak-looking, even sick, is the gold standard among Pop People and mini-celebrities. No wonder, even in middle-age and beyond, we accept that the norms of attraction are based on slimness. Few are inoculated against this perception. We look in the mirror and see someone entirely different than our real selves. It merely reflects and does not embody. It cannot project sex appeal, intelligence, charisma, humour or authority.

At the most extreme level, dysmorphics see themselves as having one or more desperate problems. They have body obsessions that they believe can only be adjusted with extreme dieting, plastic surgery or drugs. They see themselves as monsters. No matter how many times one might reassure them that they are normal and attractive, they still reject some essential part of themselves. This is a genuine disease *in the extreme*, and most of us do not have it. But there is a lesson to be learned here: try always to concentrate on the positive. If all else fails, see a doctor.

CHAPTER SEVENTEEN

Flesh

Look in the mirror and be brutally honest with yourself. For the over-fifties a number of things happen. First, you see the ghost of who you once were, though she is still in there somewhere. That person is fresh-faced and has a toned body with firm, rounder contours. You have a youthful image of yourself, and it remains in your reflection. Then follows the surprise that stares back at you. This is the you of today, the result of living and ageing. She has lines and a bit of deterioration. She may be well preserved, exercised and dieted into a reasonable condition. She may have had a bit of work done around the jaw line. Her skin may have the lustre of someone on endless HRT, but she is older, presumably wiser and a little shocked looking back at you. She is the reality of your naked body, top to toe, and you must decide how much you want to show. We are still women and have a sexuality that stays with us until the end. It is in our DNA and not to be denied.

Let us consider the moving parts: face, breasts, legs, shoulders, derrière, hands, neck, back, midriff and feet. These are commonly accepted erogenous zones that have changed in emphasis through the ages. During the Napoleonic era, women wore little muslin dresses, wetted down to show off their bosoms and legs (as in a wet T-shirt contest). The Victorian's erotic zone was the waist, constricted by tight whalebone corsets and emphasized with a rear-end bustle. The ultimate turn on for a mandarin was feet – upper-class Chinese women's feet were bound at birth (to never grow larger than a lotus blossom). Flappers in the 1920s showed their knees and the back of their necks. Breasts came back in the

1950s in an almost maternal way after the Second World War. Mini-skirts in the 1960s showed off long skinny legs. Recently, the midriff and below represent the elements of desire, graphically in some cases. No matter what the body or the fashion, however, everything begins with the face.

Face Facts

For the middle-aged woman, the issue is how to retain youthfulness, not youth. Youth is round, plump and lineless. There are new cosmetic and surgical procedures for either retaining or regaining this youthful appearance, but let us start at an easier and less invasive level.

Makeup. Let us assume that your skin is still reasonably taut, that you have good bone structure, pretty eyes and a nice neck. But you have changed. There is a papery fine look to some more mature skins, or a slightly orange-peel coarseness. It is drier all over or in places. There is a tendency to get rough patches. When you wake up in the morning, your eyes may be puffy. There is a bit of droop at the chin line and a general lack of definition. Because we have lost colour, texture and luminosity, going *au natural* is no longer an option.

We need makeup now, and the many brands that supply it can be our best friends. Makeup can give us back the illusion of a healthy glow. You need certain tools and a palette of colours to achieve a fresher face, and we can all benefit from a lesson by a professional. Take a trip to the best makeup department you know. Look at the products at several counters, speak with the assistants, resisting their blandishments until you find what you think might suit you. At this point in our lives, we do not need heavyweight makeup; acne is thankfully a thing of the past. We don't want neon effects in eye-shadow or lipstick. We want earth colours, a bit of shine, moisture and credibility. We want our skin to look smooth, toned and healthy – and when we crack a glorious smile, we don't want our makeup to crack too.

We must start with the transforming moisturizers. Every day the labs come up with a new "miracle" product. Some are better than others. Insist on trying them before you buy. The assistant will give you a sample or two if she senses you are genuinely keen, which is usually helped if you have just bought another product. Try a little on your hand. If it seems tacky or heavy in texture, reject it. If you have any known allergies or sensitivities, try it (somewhere not too obvious) overnight. Ones we like are: anything by Olay; Rene Guinot (the Rolls Royce of skincare); Natura Bise (diamond); Chantecaille (infused with natural oils and rose petals); Eve Lom, especially her all-purpose cleanser and TLC night cream; Sisley; Decleor (aromatherapy-based); and Espa's ultra-light facial oil. Cosmetic companies use expressions like "seem to," "give the feeling" and "appear to reduce fine lines," which is of course to protect themselves from violating advertising standards. They imply that their formulas will perform mini-face lifts. They cannot, but fine products can improve the condition of your skin, provide surface moisture, give a smoother feeling and provide a good base for the application of makeup.

After you have made the vital decision about which moisture-bearing product to apply on very clean skin, you need the proper foundation to compliment and even out your skin-tones. Women's faces are generally not monotone. Your cheeks may be white and your nose and chin pinker. You may be very ruddy. You might have bits of tan left on your forehead, collarbone and neck. A good foundation should be chosen in a correct light by a sympathetic consultant, keeping in mind whether your skin is still oily or has become drier. If you do not know already, learn how to apply this foundation to the parts of your face that need it, always carefully blending it in with your fingertips, a slightly damp sponge or a brush.

Professional makeup artists use a battery of tools to produce a "natural" look, and it takes time and practice. You cannot apply makeup in a hurry. Buy the best products you can afford. They are well worth the money because they go on smoothly and last. Buy a coordinating concealer (YSL makes a great one), either pencil or cream, for shadows under the eyes and around the mouth. Use your little finger or a tiny brush to pat on a dot or two, blending them well, or you will look like a panda or someone with severe anaemia. A little concealer goes a long way. Massive doses are an expensive waste, as most of the excess will have to be wiped off.

Use a portable mirror with a magnifying side and situate it in natural light so that you can see yourself properly. At night, put your makeup on under a strong electric source. There is nothing worse than thickly caked foundation in the cracks of your mouth and nose. If you have good skin, an alternative to foundation is a tinted moisturizer, which is lighter, more natural-looking and flattering in summer when you have a light tan. Lancôme and Bobbi Brown do good ones.

Are You Too Old to Blush?

Most women look a bit washed out or sallow without some colour on their cheek bones. There are different opinions as to where blusher should be applied. Some prefer it on the *pommettes* (French for "apple cheeks"), others like it higher up, as an accent near the eyes. It depends on your bone structure, but a good consultant can advise you as to what looks best. What kind of blusher should you use? If your skin is dry, the cream types blend better and look more natural. Lightly applied powder is good for oilier skins or touch-ups. Earthy shades, pinkish browns, golden pinks, pale bronzes and apricots should be sheer in texture; beware of shades that are too yellow or orange. No matter what your complexion, apply bronzers with a light hand, or you will run the risk of looking like a terracotta urn. Armani does excellent powders and liquids that give the appearance of a healthy glow; Italians do like their sun tans. English women are generally fairer, but a touch of light gold (Guerlain does a great bronze range) mimics an hour in the sun. If your skin is truly pink or even ruddy, use a correcting foundation with a bit of ivory in it, and forget the blusher. We strongly recommend investing in a large, soft, rounded brush, which ensures a light dusting of bronze highlight in the right amount. These are expensive, but with proper care (wash occasionally in mild shampoo and air dry) will last forever. You do not want a solid streak of brownish powder on your cheeks that looks more like war paint than natural healthy skin.

Finally, if you're seeking a consultant, look for a woman: men can be brilliant, but women will always seem more empathetic.

The Eyes Have It

Always wear mascara, whatever you do, unless you have an allergy. If you do have bad reactions, you might consider having your lashes tinted at a salon. Wear black or brown mascara, never navy, and separate the lashes with a small brush or comb. Use eye-shadow in neutral tones; avoid burgundy, cerise, peach and turquoise. Sales people will always encourage you to buy these colours because "they bring out the blue in your eyes." Be careful. On middle-aged eyes these can end up making you look like a rescue dog having a curiously challenging day or someone who has suffered a recent painful loss. If anyone tries to sell you vivid shades of pink, blue or viridian, move away in a hurry, with or without a mumbled regret.

Grey shadow can be a bit draining and too much like how we feel sometimes. Better to choose from the taupe, slate and coffee tones, depending on the colour of your skin and eyes. Pale peachy beiges and browns are almost universally flattering. If you have very deep-set eyes, you hardly require shadow. You might do better with a bit of light foundation on your eyes and smoky-brown pencil at the lash line. Once you have bought a new eye-shadow, layer it lightly on the lid, starting from the centre of the eye and blending outward. Never apply shadow in the inner corner, which brings the widest-set eyes closer together. Use a fine-haired brush to soften the edges. There was a time for all of us when we could wear great splodges of colour, buckets of makeup in any colour, false eyelashes, bright-pink lipstick and look as cute as a bug. That was then. This is now.

Are You a Lipstick Collector?

Do you hang on to lipsticks for dear life and store them away for years like fine wines? Guess what, they are not collector's items. In fact, they age faster than you do, so the first step to a new and better look is to turf most of them out. Forget the dark browns and intense plums. Throw out those incandescent scarlets, iridescent tangerines, muddy mauves and bright mandarins. Forget sugar pink, hot pink and that awful pasty nude colour worn with a pencilled dark outline. Coromandel Red is the devil.

Once you have rid yourself of the dried-up, extraneous lipsticks you probably never wear anyway, your mind is clear to buy two or three fresh new colours. We recommend those from Chantecaille, Guerlain, Lancôme, Estée Lauder and Bobbi Brown, who seem to specialize in the kinds of colours we can all wear. Try browny pinks, rusty neutral reds and bronze tones. Buy a clear gloss in a tube or wand (nicer than a pot) and just apply a smear over colour. Heavy gooey gloss is a major turn-off and gets on your teeth. A little bronze glitter in your gloss is a healthy-looking summer option.

Very dark lipstick emphasizes facial hair, however sparse and bleached-away yours might be, and little lines, so stay away from it. Bright-red lipstick can be worn if blotted down; you do not want your lipstick smeared on your bicuspids. You could use a natural-toned lip-liner, but delicately. There is nothing worse or more pathetic-looking than a heavy outlined mouth – and no lip tattooing ever. The magic of a properly applied lip-liner is the suggestion of a child's defined mouth. The line helps to hold the lipstick colour and creates the illusion of full-ness, as long as you can control your desire to paint on a full mouth that nearly extends to your nostrils. Try the Joan Crawford look in front of the bedroom mirror late at night with a full pout if you must. Throw on a feather boa while you are at it and strike a sexy pose. It will make a great little show for your husband, but never go out of the house with it on like that.

Everyone has her makeup routine: evaluate yours, and change it if you do not think it is doing anything for you. You must regularly clean out your makeup drawer. Also, do not keep old pressed powder with grimy puffs. Buy a pretty new compact. A woman of any age putting on a bit of lipstick and powder is a bit erotic, so make the most of it.

The Defining Brow

Our concept of eyebrow shapes is often dictated by fashion: thin, thick, arched, straight, bushy, combed, dark or light, not to mention the vagaries of Hollywood styles and celebrity culture. If you should be watching a late-night movie starring the great Greta Garbo, pay particular attention to the shape of her eyebrows. They were a remarkable frame for her magnificent eyes and as beautiful today as they were then.

Today's eyebrow shape is natural-looking – neat and well groomed. Many of us, however, have overplucked, to put it mildly, and eyebrows do not grow back the way they once were. Our advice is to go to a professional to re-establish a good shape (there are "threading" specialists in London's Harvey Nichols and Fenwicks). Once this is done, you can maintain your eyebrows yourself, using slanted tweezers, a good magnifying mirror and a steady hand. Be careful, you don't want to poke out your eye, or take more hairs than necessary, a common occurrence. With an eyebrow pencil in a lighter shade (never ginger unless you are a redhead), hold your forehead taut and fill in any patchy sections of the brow with feathery strokes, following the natural arch. If you never had an arch, now is the time to get one. Use a tiny brush to smooth hairs and blend together.

If you don't like the results, cream it off and start again. It needs a little practice if you have never done it before. Say no to black, even if you have very dark hair; use a charcoal pencil instead. Those wonderful dark brows you have favoured since the days of mini-skirts and Sassoon haircuts give a Groucho-esque, rather furious look now. Avoid like malaria.

CHAPTER EIGHTEEN

Skin: Change and the Illusion of Change

A good facial clears away the cobwebs both dermatological and emotional. A bad facial, however, is like bad sex: better to have none at all. Maybe you are not comfortable with people touching your skin. If there is any excessive tugging or stretching, it will do you little harm but no real good either. An expert practitioner is virtually worth her weight in plastic surgeons; there are marvellous skin experts out there. Often your friends will have some special private person that they use and, if you are close, might be willing to share the name.

Once you have found a good cosmetician, stick with her (or him) and have regular treatments. Your skin will be cleaner, fresher, invigorated, and the massage will help firm up facial muscles. Fruit acid peels and cathiodermie are excellent for removing dead skin and adding moisture, but be careful if you have sensitivities. Always discuss any concerns or allergies with the consultant. Many women feel pressured to buy the products after the treatment, so a nice way to deal with this is to mention beforehand that you would like to buy one product at the end. They will always hand you a list (especially on your first visit), but you will have already made it clear that you are not ready to buy the whole range until you have tried one at home first.

Alas, many of us develop dermatitis as time goes by. Just when teenage acne becomes a distant memory, we become afflicted by dry red patches and puffiness around the eyes as a matter of course. Have the consultant take a history of your skin before they recommend one of their products. If you are worried, ask to try a bit in the crook of your arm. An adverse reaction will probably appear in an hour or two. These products are expensive, and you don't want to make a mistake.

If you do not wish to spend the money, go home, whip up an egg yolk, a slice of avocado and some olive oil in the blender, and it will probably have a similar moisturizing effect – though will be a whole lot messier. And if you prefer to give yourself a facial, which is never entirely as effective because most of us don't have the time or patience, try cleansers and masques sold by Decleor, Clarins, Rene Guinot, Aveda, Givenchy and Eve Lom. Facials do not produce instant miracles. They are not a substitute for your own personal vigilance. But periodic facials will have positive regenerative effects, help hold moisture in your clean and toned skin and make you feel very good indeed.

Exfoliation of Skin on the Body

We can exfoliate our skin in the shower with a rough towelling wash-cloth, a soft brush or a loofah. A number of new products for the body have arrived on the market, such as salt, sugar and rice-grain scrubs, and scents ranging from fig, cucumber and crème brûlée to seaweed and flowers. You can smell like a rose or a salad, as you wish. As you would use a moisturiser on your face, do the same with your body. Clarins, Jo Malone, Laura Mercier, Coudray, Sisley, Jergens, Ponds and Olay make wonderful body potions. We love Dr Hauschka's Lavender Oil. Run a bath, put in less than a capful of bath oil under the tap and relax. If you jog through Richmond Park with your greyhound, or are planning a trip to the American countryside anytime soon, you might like to know that Skin so Soft by Avon (it smells of eucalyptus) is reputed to be a known mosquito and tick deterrent.

In addition to product research and self-renewal, at our age we must have access to a good dermatologist to inspect the skin on our faces as well as on our bodies. The sun exposure we had as children and young adults – remember those aluminium reflectors – can actually change our cellular structure. In extreme cases, we may have developed precancerous cells or even the big C. Most of these tags, spots, warts, lesions, keratoses and growths of all sizes and shapes are easy to deal with, but it is vital to check regularly to discover small problems before they become big ones. Continually inspect your skin, know yourself and identify change. We are so hung up on our outward appearance that we can miss or deny something that is shouting out for attention, such as a rough patch or a new dark brown dot.

Plastic Surgery, Botox, Fillers and Lasers

Physically altering your body using surgical procedures is based on individual needs and societal norms. There are whole cities, like Los Angeles, where most people think nothing of chopping and changing themselves as a matter of course. Their friends do it, so why not? Then there are people in the public eye – mainly celebrities – who believe their jobs depend on youthful skin and a chiselled jawline. As Julie Christie put it when she finally submitted to the knife, people in Hollywood who were older than she was were beginning to look younger, which in her view was an impossible situation for a working actress. In corporate America, many men and women choose to have a discreet eye job or neck tightening for what they believe makes them appear more vital and competitive.

Psychologically, some of us simply cannot cope with the deterioration we see in the mirror – wrinkles, fine lines and sun damage. For some, surgery is a positive decision. A good face-lift – there are many revolutionary techniques today – can be a fresh start in life. Interestingly, very pretty women do not seem to gain as much from them as their plainer sisters. Perhaps a face-lift changes one a bit too drastically to retain the soft charms of an attractive face. Some surgeries can imbue a person with a surreal aspect, as if the face does not match the hands and body skin. Still, many opt for it, and only one rule should apply: go to the very best doctor you can find. There are no short-cuts or budget lifts (though some people swear by operations in Mexico and Thailand), unless you win a place on one of the television make-over programmes.

Botox works, especially on the lines on your forehead, but there are many cases of disappointment or partial paralysis of the eye lids if things go wrong. One friend claims she developed rheumatoid arthritis shortly after she started Botox treatments. It's important to remember that in order to retain the good effects you must keep doing it. Frankly, we find it a bit scary.

Chemical peels for acne scars are very effective. Every day, in every way, fuelled by society's youth worship, the medical profession finds new methods for improving reality. Only you, however, can decide if surgically transforming yourself will gain you what you really want. Counselling can be useful too, though frankly there is no substitute for a strong ego and an abiding interest. Get one if you can.

CHAPTER NINETEEN

Hair

We are not hair consultants, but we do know that clean, well-cut hair and up-to-date roots are a must. Remember Blondie in the 1980s, with her highlights jumping out of black partings? She was *sooo* cool. Blondie is well past sixty now, and if she showed her roots today they would be grey. So keep a weather eye. Here are some good rules to follow.

Older hair needs to be lighter in tone. Do not go darker. Do not try to hang onto your original colour because *you* are not your original colour. Just as your hair has faded, so has your skin. Go to the best salon you can afford and take their advice. Most good colourists will be honest. They will tell you what they can and cannot do. Bring pictures, even though it can be difficult to find appropriate ones because the models are usually underage. Don't be afraid to ask questions or give your opinion. Make a joint decision and then relax.

Blonde or blonder is the easiest to go for, but be careful because on the wrong skin tones, with the wrong colour eyes, it can wash you right out. Also it can be brassy, yellow, greenish or fall out from over-processing. It can look cheap and brittle, which is why a first-rate salon is a necessary expense. Some of the best places in London are Daniel Galvin, Toni & Guy, John Frieda, Michaeljohn, Real, Neville, Daniel Hersheson and Jo Hansford. If you want to maintain your brown, red or brunette tones, consult a good salon and ask to get the most natural-looking effect, which usually involves several tones rather than a solid colour and can be expensive and time-consuming. If you have always coloured your hair yourself, stay abreast of new products and looks and adjust it a bit from time to time.

Grey is not pretty, don't kid yourself. It is ageing and draining because your greying hair becomes a different texture, often wiry and unmanageable. Some women, however have colouring that is incredibly vivid, and they can do grey. We know a few who are positively stunning, but they have dark skin and eyes and no traces of yellow in their hair. If you like your white hair, by all means use a rinse to eliminate yellow tones, but avoid Dame Edna lavenders or blues. If you are one of the lucky ones, and grey hairs are late to come to you, wait before doing anything drastic. You might look interesting with a streak of white or two. Again, ask advice before you consider having a tint or highlights.

Products on less-than-perfect hair can be utterly transformative. Think about hair wax, glosses, anti-frizz serums, deep conditioners and hairsprays. These are not just for the teenager's bathroom cabinet, these products help give the illusion of healthy hair, which means movement, silkiness and separate strands, not helmets of fixed-coloured cement. Every time you blow-dry your hair you are damaging it, so it's good to have an occasional professional conditioning treatment. If you do your own hair, use a deep-conditioning product at home. Apply the conditioner after a shampoo and sit with a damp towel on your head for a half-hour. You can polish your toenails while you wait, or read a few chapters of *The Decline of the Roman Empire*. If your hair is very curly and you long for straight, throw out your old straighteners and invest in good ceramic ones, available from your local hairdresser. They don't damage the hair shaft and heat instantly (but watch your ears). Use a specially formulated hair moisturiser to prevent excessive drying. They are amazing for transforming frizz into a silken curtain of hair.

If your hair is straight as a stick already, lotions, mousses, gels and thickeners all give body and volume. The biochemist is our best friend. Aveda makes a great series of natural shampoos and conditioners that work like a dream, especially the Mint and Rosemary conditioner, which is practically good enough to eat. Try products by Frédéric Fekkai, Toni & Guy, John Frieda (especially for frizz) and Pantene. Stay away from cheap brands sold on supermarket shelves, as they have far too much alcohol content and are sold for mass consumption.

A few other tips: use a covered elastic band, always, if you pull your hair back. Don't use cheap hair grips or clips because they pull your hair out. We cannot afford to lose a single strand. Sun destroys hair colour, so if it is practical, cover your head by wearing a straw hat. Or tie a scarf on your bag that you can pop on your head when the rays are stronger.

Haircuts

Having your hair cut can be one of life's most traumatic events. We can all remember going into a hairdresser in a mad mood, saying "Cut it all off." In our youth this usually happened after seeing a movie in which the heroine was gamine (like Mia Farrow in *Rosemary's Baby*), and had her hair chopped in little points, or in the 1960s, was cut geometrically. Vidal Sassoon launched thousands of young women with a squared-off fringe, short back and sides.

In "Bernice Bobs Her Hair," a seminal short story by F. Scott Fitzgerald, the eponymous heroine has her long beautiful hair cut off in a boyish bob in response to a dare by her bitchy cousin. In the mirror she contemplates with rue her new short-haired self and sees that she has lost some of her femininity, which has been replaced by an androgynous self. One night, she exacts a revenge by chopping off her cousin's thick blonde braid as she sleeps. In the last scene, Bernice leaves her aunt's house, in full moonlight, carrying a carelessly packed suitcase, running helter skelter for the train station. As she runs off the front porch, she hurls the severed braid against the door in defiance. Two things have happened: Bernice has been shorn of one important aspect of her female self, long hair. She has lost something precious, but assertion and aggressiveness have taken its place. Never again will she play the victim in someone else's game. A tentative self-confidence has been born out of that bobbed hair. She will renew herself. She doesn't need her long hair to become the person she wants to be. She is free.

Many of us have tasted this liberation when we have taken a decision to radically alter our hair style, freeing and reinventing ourselves. People notice a striking new hair cut, question it and respond to you differently. They might even expect you to be a different kind of a person, and all that from a haircut. So if everyday is a Bad Hair day, if it is limp and unresponsive to the many potions that we would advocate, perhaps it is time to sharpen up and chop. If it is wiry and ill-tempered and needs constant discipline at the hairdresser's to get it smooth, this too should make you rethink your hairstyle. Short hair requires a great deal of maintenance and must be cut regularly; colouring will require even more vigilance.

Long hair, when you have been used to a wash-and-wear haircut, requires a change of thinking as well. Very long hair on a middle-aged woman is possible if it has a beautiful texture and is worn in a distinctive style, up and away from the shoulders and face. It is a very sophisticated look, however, but might just be your "signature." You can find wonderful hair accessories and pins in tortoiseshell, gold, silk, velvet and fake jewels. Do not, as a rule, wear it flowing down your back, and try not to pull it too tightly. You could look severe and strained.

A new haircut is a statement, so after fifty be very careful about changing yourself radically. You have to be able to live up to this new look, which might require a change of dress, makeup, jewellery, the lot. But sometimes change is necessary to reveal another dimension. Hair does grow back, as our mothers used to console us when we arrived home from the salon after trying to look like Twiggy but emerged looking like a shaved rabbit instead.

If you are constantly frustrated by what you see on your head, or if the thought of change occupies your conversation more than it should, then consider a different look. It is a thought process akin to: do you think I should lose weight? If you keep asking that question, it is reasonable to assume that you do. You are a mature woman, and if your hair is your glory, keep it strong and healthy, but retain your dignity. Most of us stick to modified or compromised cuts, taking hair length up and down like yoyos. These haircuts do not make a statement or a real change, and that is often quite enough. If you are truly bored with your hair, however, bite the bullet and go for it, just once.

CHAPTER TWENTY

The Chest, *Poitrine*, Cleavage, Bosoms

They say there are three kinds of men – breast men, leg men and those who like the rear. What do bosoms do except scare us to death, medically? They either sit there heavily or bounce and jiggle. They are either solid or flabby. They come in all shapes and sizes, and depending on the message you wish to send, you either hide or flash them. There are women who are proud of theirs, plan their wardrobes around them and consider them the first line of offense in the attractions arsenal. For these women and for those who could not care less about their breasts, we offer some guidance.

There is nothing more ageing than crepey skin on mature embonpoint. Cleavage in middle age is a bit of a conundrum. Women have breasts, but how can we get the most out of them as we grow older? You must care for your breasts as you do for the rest of you. First, be honest with yourself. How is your skin? Is it freckly from the sun, wrinkled, spotty, parchment-dry or smooth and creamy? Are their shapes droopy, perky, massive, flattened, saggy, baggy or nifty? Do the upper halves appear as if they are missing? To get the best take on your bosom status, try on a range of your bras, sweaters, blouses and evening tops, and decide whether you like what you see. Plunging cleavage is meretricious, overwhelming – even threatening – and young women can do it much better. Older women with an abundance of cleavage look like they are trying too hard.

Ensure that the skin on your face, neck and chest go together. One may be much older-looking than the other and create an alarming contrast, especially if you have had plastic surgery. If you have good shoulders and firm skin, a bustier is youthful and complimentary. Deep-v, plunging necklines are too obvious. Frontless or backless dresses are *de trop*, except in high summer at a resort where everyone is doing the same thing and you won't stand out. The young, smoother ones will be noticed first, and you will just benefit from the cool air. If you do dare to bare, by all means keep a little sweater, tiny jacket, capelet or silk shawl handy. Open a few shirt buttons and make sure you have some pretty lace underneath. Unsupported breasts are acceptable if you are very small, love your comfort and do not mind people looking in. If you are wearing a fitted, low-cut dress, not transparent and that has a certain measure of lift, you can go without (or "commando-style," as it is sometimes indelicately put). You do not need to show off much to be feminine and elegant. Modesty is a virtue and creates intrigue for the curious. If you like to flaunt it, bring a man along for protection and expect the odd remark.

Time to Talk Brassières

You have probably tried on hundreds of bras in dozens of styles – from teenage training models, nursing and sports bras, to that ultimate icon, the Wonderbra – forever seeking a good fit. The perfect bra is supportive, comfortable, uplifting and pretty, and does not cost the earth. Be assured that this bra does *not* exist, and you will have to compromise. If it is gorgeous, sexy and fits, it will probably be very expensive. Even then, it might tug, pull, itch, hurt and annoy. As a breast doctor put it recently, breast tissue turns to fat over time. Even small-breasted women, especially those of us who have breast-fed or jogged, are in need of support.

Do you know what size you are? Women's breasts change all the time, possibly growing one or two cup sizes with age (especially if you're taking HRT). One breast may be bigger than the other, if only imperceptibly. You must get measured properly. Like mammograms, this should be done regularly. The manufacturer and the width of your back can also determine cup size, hence 32C can be 34B, depending on the brand. We believe the best shape to aim for is rounded and natural, with a bit of uplift – not rigid or resembling coffee cups. Anything that looks natural takes more effort and costs extra. A cheap bra gives you a prepressed, manipulated look that defies good clothes and biology.

Are You Wired?

Breast doctors are noncommittal about wires because there is some debate about whether they are a health hazard. On the fashion front, however, we suggest a simple, lightweight wire that does not bind and supports softly. A bit of padding is up to you. Bras with thick pads, heavy straps, too many hooks and liquid-filled inner pockets make a bad statement under clothes and should be avoided. You can afford to be a little wilder in the evenings if you want a bosomy look, by showing a bit of ribbon and lace.

Large-breasted woman should not be terrorized into buying bras that make them look three times their size. We do not care what the saleswoman says about proper fitting. Insist on something that minimizes and softens your look. How many times have you fallen for the "proper fit" game and wound up with enormous, foam-filled mountains on your chest? Always bring a T-shirt with you when trying undergarments on to see out the effect.

We love Hanro for comfort, ease and youthful style. Try Erès, the pinnacle of off-the-peg bras, although they are pricey. Lejaby are a French brand that are ultra-feminine, in sizes up to the maximum and come with matching knickers. For flirty, lacy, show-off bras you cannot beat La Perla, keeping in mind that they are for the smaller – not necessarily younger – person. Their beautiful colours and wonderful fabrics are to die for, but their shapes can be a bit unaccommodating. Buy one with matching French knickers before you go on holiday.

Consider the ultimate retailer for bras on the High Street – the one and only Marks & Spencer. They make good copies of every brand in every size (statistically, women are getting larger), but they can fall short on the comfort factor because their mass-produced fabrics are less luxurious. If you can tolerate a bit of discomfort, they are good value. Calvin Klein, Warners and Donna Karan are in there with the latest looks.

A word about care: never put your good bras in the washing machine, especially the ones with under-wires. Instead, try washing them by hand in the sink using a little shampoo.

Camisoles and Silky Vests

What a sexy thing to keep you warm and pretty. Pink, beige, taupe, peach, baby-blue, black and lace-trimmed, they can be worn under jackets, cardigans and blazers as alternatives to blouses and T-shirts. Designers such as Moschino make outerwear in underwear shapes. Beware of these as they can be overpriced and fit badly. The best silky camisoles are found on every street corner in Paris. In London, you can find very lovely ones at Fenwick's and the lingerie departments of larger stores. Wear your pretty lace under the strictest suit. Pretty lingerie is what French women know from birth.

The Midriff

Now we must move to the body parts that are more of a problem. Unless you are a performer before a Cuban rhythm section, forget showing the midriff. That's right, we know it has been fashion-forward – Madonna did it, Beyonce is doing it, Christina Aguilera does it, but it is over now. For us, it has been over for years. You may have a beautiful body, a mid-section like a kettle drum or a six-pack, but just forget it. This rule should only be broken on a golden tropical beach – just you, the sand, surf, your best friend (possibly male), a beautifully cut Liza Bruce bikini, plenty of factor 20 and a few frigate birds flying overhead. Day-time or night-time, in the big city, midriff is a no-no, no matter what the provocation. This is the wrong erogenous zone for you.

CHAPTER TWENTY-ONE

Hands

If your hands are less than flower-like because you have sculpted, banged out endless études by Lizst, weeded like a demon or forgotten to use Marigold rubber gloves for the washing up – do not despair. Your hands may be small and square, or large and ham-like. You may not have perfect oval nails but fragile, weak ones. You may be a recovering nail-biter. Although there are, as yet, no plastic surgery procedures for nail augmentation or finger lengthening (we live in hope), there nevertheless exist some genuine solutions to make your problem hands look more elegant and feminine. It's worth finding the right solution because fake nails can fall off, extensions encourage fungus underneath and their shovel-like, squared-off tips are not always the most attractive shapes.

First rule, as mother and nanny always reminded us: clean under your nails. Even if you do not have a hand model's hands, and you spend a great deal of time at the potter's wheel, yours can be clean, soft and efficient-looking. They can express strength *and* artistry.

In order to guard against freckles and brown blotches, scrupulously protect your hands from the sun by wearing SPF factor 20. Wear gloves when you garden, drive, and for protection and warmth in winter. You could find short cotton pique or kidskin gloves for spring and summer, but that would be a retro statement and would have to be done with humour.

Treat rings as an extension of your personality (see the jewellery section) and wear a signature ring. Big mega-amethysts, single-stone citrines, smoky quartz and coral make a great statement, even if you have short fingers, and are relatively inexpensive. Think Ringo.

You can make a personal statement about yourself by using hand gestures. Movie stars of the smoking era did just that, with the whole cigarette routine – the lighting, the holding, the puffing and the posing. We have to make do with chunky bracelets, interesting rings and good-looking pens to show off slim wrists and great nails. It is the one regrettable feature of giving up smoking…it was so sexy.

Nails benefit from cuticle repair and creams and should be polished or buffed to a pink glow. Be vigilant about your cuticles, keeping them trim and neat. Use Mavala cuticle cream or Linda Rose nail and cuticle serum to keep the skin around your nails soft and the nail-bed healthy. Try not to dig into the "moon," as this will damage the nail. Do not file your nails square, it makes the edges weak. Do not file to a point, same problem. Do not sport ultra-red or dark-brown nail polish, unless you have beautiful hands. We envy all women who can take a French manicure or have crystals embedded, but we advise sticking to a simpler look. Keep your nails all the same length. This would seem rational, but it surprises us how many women nurture three or four nails when one or two have broken off. If you prize the length of your nails, have a professional apply some fake ones, but only while your damaged ones grow back.

Manicures can produce healthy rounded shapes. Have them regularly, bearing in mind that not every manicurist is good. A recommendation from a friend is best. For a youthful look, keep nails medium length, polished in soft pink, rusty red or nude – if in doubt, pale and clear is best; leave the fluorescent and Dragon Lady blood-reds to others. If you do love your reds, however, remember that they are high maintenance, so ensure they are never chipped or peeling. So tacky. Use hand lotion frequently (collect tiny, free samples and put them in your handbag so you can apply while out and about). Look into Everlasting Nails, a special polish that can be applied professionally at many nailbars. It dries instantly, comes in a range of colours, including "French," and lasts for weeks.

We repeat: DO WEAR GLOVES. They are so *now*. Gloves should fit snugly and be very clean, especially if they are a light colour. Old, creased and greasy gloves cannot be restored – just throw them out. The best place in the world to buy gloves is on Paris's Rue de Rivoli. Proprietors will show you beautiful kidskins and suedes in every colour of the rainbow, that will break your heart. Your size will be fitted perfectly. Like the softest second skin and sensual to the touch, suede gloves are the ultimate pleasure, and the colours are subtle, even if they are the sharpest yellowish-greens or pinks. And don't forget that taking off a glove can be one of the arts of seduction that never fails. Think Rita Hayworth in *Gilda*.

CHAPTER TWENTY-TWO

The Derrière

Every woman's biggest problem: the behind, the sitting down, the bottom, the butt – has anyone of a certain age ever looked at herself in the mirror and honestly said, "I love my rear-end" or "I adore my backside?" It would be rare indeed to hear a woman say to her husband or best friend when she is trying on a trim skirt or, worse, a pair of trousers, "Don't you think that my bottom looks too small?" Have you ever felt insecure because you thought your bottom looked too narrow, too lean, too uplifted, too tight, too taut, too much like a pair of apricots as opposed to twin casaba melons? Impossible, except perhaps in Brazil where everyone has bottom implants. No matter how slim and well-preserved the woman, it is a fact of life that we hate our rear-ends. They are always too big.

So what to do with this bodypart that makes us crazy, has launched a thousand diets, cellulite creams and exercise regimes, that created a market for girdles and corsets in the 1950s and control pantyhose since then, this thing that men love to fondle, grab, pinch and generally admire? The cutest girls in the world hate their rears, so what hope have we? Well, help is on the way.

Take a deep breath. Take a good, long look in a rear-view mirror. Every older woman has dimples. Every older woman has a permanent press crease under her cheeks. It looks enormous in the mirror, resting in all its bifurcated glory. Now, look at the side view. Not so bad perhaps. Try to remember that most people looking at you, see your front *and* sides. That is the good news. But your bottom is actually a by-product of genes, age, gravity and years of being sat on. Imagine what your face would look like if it got the same wear and tear.

So what can you do about it? You could exercise, do water aerobics, Pilates and clench your buttocks tightly in a variety of dancer's exercises, à la the legendary Lotte Berk. You could diet and lose some weight at the same time. You could wear a supporting garment. You could choose your clothes with discretion and good sense, concentrating on the parts of yourself that you actually like. If you cannot cope with your fatty deposits another minute, you could opt for liposuction. Lots of women are doing it. It is expensive, but it can work miracles as long as you do not overeat and put the weight right back on. We have heard that the fat tends to migrate elsewhere, so discuss this with a good plastic surgeon. There are, however, less drastic approaches, and they all have to do with finding the right *fit*.

Beyond Bottoms

You may not be perfect, but who is? So let us start with trousers. First, it is fine to have a close fit over the buttocks. It is even desirable to avoid an unforgiving, middle-aged look in jeans and trousers. There is nothing worse than baggy, saggy trousers or, conversely, having them pull across the crotch and hips. So, do not worry too much about the size of your rear, what is vital is the way your trousers *fit* from waist to lower hip. If that appears smooth and properly tailored, the back end will look neat and trimmer. This requires patient experimentation with several different brands, and finding a label that suits you – once found, stick to it like your best friend.

Many women's bodies do not conform to established sizes (see the "Disproportionates" section earlier), and it might be necessary to go up or down a size, or to have the waist taken in or out, as necessary. Always insist on seeing the shop's alterations person, to pin the excess or explain how the garment should be let out. Your local dry-cleaner might be able to handle this task but it is better to demand the professional services of the shop – before you pay. If you have never done this, now is the time to learn. Once you are properly fitted, most of your aggravation will disappear as you contemplate your puckerless bottom view.

So many of our miseries come from bad fit. Skirts are much the same. Insist that the rear end fits smoothly into the hollow of the back and falls closely over the hips. The waist should allow for breathing and eating. If it is too tight, insist on having it eased. Dresses present the same challenges, and worse. Manufacturers have an ideal shape that they size up and up. If you are not that specific shape – no matter what size you are – you will never be able to just step into that brand. Be demanding. If there is no tailor on hand, and no one about to pin the garment for you correctly, do not buy it. But too much alteration risks losing the original line. If you prefer straight skirts, and the one you are trying on is an A-line, no amount of adjustment will make it right.

Colour does not matter as long as the garment fits. Anyone can choose black, one colour – jacket and skirt – that deceives the eye and creates a sense of unity and proportion. Light colours on top and dark on bottom minimize the lower half. Long jackets cover a multitude of sins. If your rear-end juts out, be sure that the bottom half of the jacket does not pull, or that the flap at the back is not sticking out; you are not after a bustle effect. A short jacket will emphasize the length of your legs, and a medium-length jacket will appear to reduce the size of your rear, to half. Small patterns can assist in creating a pleasing proportion: a neat plaid or subtle check on a jacket over a plain coloured skirt draws the eye upwards. Conversely, if you worry about your rear, avoid prints, polka-dots, stripes and zig-zags on your lower half. Plain colours are the most minimizing. We love man-tailored suits in men's fabrics – pin-stripes, Prince of Wales plaids, houndstooth checks and lightweight tweeds. They tailor well and play the masculine-feminine gender game that we love.

When is the derrière a desirable and attractive focal point for us? The answer to that question is, almost never. If you have a great body, good legs, terrific posture and were once a dancer, maybe. If you are comfortable in a G-string, by all means wear black stove-pipe trousers. Your bottom could be a joy for people to remember. Just bear in mind that they will, eventually, come round to your front view.

CHAPTER TWENTY-THREE

Teeth

D id you know that as we age our ability to keep our teeth clean naturally with our own saliva diminishes? Little children do not have permanent specks of parsley on their teeth. The flow of saliva keeps their mouths clean. And it might be a shock to know that saliva gets thicker as we get older. Little green bits get stuck. So check your teeth in the same mirror you use to powder your nose. Bleaching teeth is a popular way to brighten your smile and is done at the dentist with laser light and topped up at home with bleaching trays and gel. Floss regularly with Oral B unwaxed mint-flavoured tape (as recommended by dentists) and use an electric toothbrush with a built-in water jet.

Make friends with your dental hygienist because you should be seeing him or her four times a year, at least. In addition to the superficial, considerable advances have been made in cosmetic dentistry. No doubt you have been a bit surprised to see one of your old school mates with braces on her teeth. Even at our age, orthodonture is possible and often advisable: new braces are nearly invisible. But even without orthodonture, gaps can be corrected and smiles transformed with veneer facings and convincing crowns. The trick is to get a white that is not too startling. People make the mistake of wanting a super-white smile, which looks unrealistic, if not surreal. Go for a subtle, slightly darker shade (there is a white "colour" chart ranging from nearly olive to dazzling). You will look natural, not as though you are displaying a set of matching porcelain dishes in your mouth. If you are conscious of your breath, perhaps you are eating the wrong things. Discuss your diet with a nutritionist.

CHAPTER TWENTY-FOUR

Let's Leg It

S ome sage man once said that you should study the legs of your girl's mother as they will be the last parts to go. In our era this may still have relevance, as there seems little one can do about legs other than diet and exercise. Other parts of us can be dealt with cosmetically or surgically. (On the subject of varicose veins, if yours are unsightly, painful and itchy and cannot be managed without support hose, see your doctor. Today's methods for removal and control are far advanced from yesteryear.)

On the positive side, naked legs are sexy if they are toned, tanned, shapely, shod in high heels and without blemish. No spots, varicose veins, dimples, wrinkles or dry spots. The very young can go without stockings and wear very short skirts and shorts. Although the skin ages on the body more slowly than on the face and hands, over-fifties should wear tights, get a St Tropez tan, have their dermatologists burn off spots and look at their skirt lengths with a gimlet eye. Naked or covered, legs must always be well groomed. If you go barelegged in the summer, make sure you have fake tan applied. If you do it yourself, use a very good product. You do not want that jaundiced look that you get from an unpredictable tube of self-tanning lotion, such as the one hiding in your cupboard from your trip to Italy two years ago. Self-tan is not tanning protection so remember to cream on your 15+ SPF when you sit in the sun.

Make sure your legs are waxed and immaculate. With depilation, there are good operatives and bad. The best ones work deftly and quickly, with little more than a slight stinging sensation. Inexperienced or downright bad operators, however, can leave you bruised, burnt or bleeding. There are entire ranges of techniques: hot waxing, waxing with strips of linen, cold wax, sugaring, threading and anti-allergy methods for ultra-sensitive skins. Waxing leaves skin smoother than shaving, prevents regrowth for up to five weeks and conditions by removing the top layer of dry skin. Hair removal goes back to the ancient Egyptians, who used scallop shells as tweezers to take out hair, one by one. No doubt women then had a bit more time on their hands. Hairless was best then, as now, what with their sheer linen togas and low-slung kilts. Bikini wax is a must if you are in a bathing suit. The "Brazilian," or so-called "landing strip," is a bit brutal but very modern.

Stockings and Tights
If you are a committed garter-belt women, then by all means wear stockings. Some women love the airiness and find it free and sexy. We, however, believe it is a throwback to corsets and foot-binding. The garter-belt is bulky, ruins the line of a snug skirt and includes the palaver of either wearing bikini panties underneath or French knickers over. Perhaps the sexy garter-belt and matching accoutrements should be confined to the bedroom, complete with satin mules with feathery pom poms for those little love games.

If you feel that your legs are not your strong point, limit how much you show by wearing cropped trousers or diaphanous skirts. A bit of gauze or chiffon can be amazingly flattering. We love naked legs under trousers, but it is not for everyone. Some can benefit from a little powder in their shoes or boots, others need socks.

Tights are warmer and give you a seamless line, but give the rear no definition so you may appear more monolithic from behind, as if you were wearing a girdle. Tights under skirts are fundamental except in boiling weather. For us, there should be two types: opaque and very sheer. Opaque tights in black, dark brown or anthracite-grey create a long elegant leg, a good silhouette, are young and modern and – as an added bonus – usually snag-resistant. Avoid bright colours like red or blue or you will look like a grouse. Opaque tights look best with high-heeled shoes because there is a contrast between sensible and sensual. Sheer tights, on the other hand, in a nude colour matching your skin tone are feminine, grown-up and definitely sexy. Avoid sheers that are too dark, which render your legs a funny colour and show the first sign of a ladder; or too pale, which makes all but the skinniest legs look thicker. Wear tan hose in summer only, over a tan. Avoid at all costs heavy, flesh-coloured hose, especially with shiny lycra, which look like a surgical treatment for varicose veins or attract attention to every imperfection, from bony to fat knees, to less-than-delicate ankles. Please do not be tempted by the ghastly idea that stocking manufacturers put forth every so often: patterned tights. At best, with tiny polka dots, they do nothing much; at worst, with large meandering fuzzy patterns, they make legs look grotesque. Bright, patterned tights are for the very young during their experimental years. If you must indulge in a bit of folly, fishnet hose – freezing, of course – can be sexy and cute in either black or nude.

From legs we proceed to feet, which should be dealt with regularly by a chiropodist or a talented beautician. Rough skin, potential corns and calluses should be smoothed away often, not just for beauty but for the foot's health. Older feet are bonier, hence painful, and need TLC. There is hardly anything more ageing than scaly feet with poorly maintained nails and cuticles. Keep your pumice stone handy and a rich cream to massage onto heels and soles, but do not walk on the bathroom floor without soft slippers after creaming your feet or you might slip. In open-toed sandals, your feet, cleaned and smooth and with bright-red polish can be feminine, sexy and aesthetically pleasing at any age.

There is one part of the body that may be too thin (we thought it could never be): the bottom of the foot. Be prepared for pain over time. Buy slim-line shoe inserts from Dr Scholl's to cushion your feet. Don't just sit there. Keep moving.

SHOP UNTIL YOU DROP

CHAPTER TWENTY-FIVE

Sales

The Chanel invitation arrives on a stiff white card, expensively printed and full of promise. The store shuts for a week and new stock is hidden away. All of last season's models and rejects are trotted out for the customer, even though steady clients have already had first refusal on sale items. It is also likely that the regular Chanel customer has bought, from the collection's first arrival, all the things that she wanted, hence the most desirable sizes and styles are long gone. What is available, often brought in from other branches, are pieces that were possibly produced too abundantly or proved unpopular. Perhaps these pieces were impractical. For the fashion prima donna, they are "so last collection," so they need to find a new audience.

Nevertheless, if you have nothing to do on a Chanel sale day (and that includes other designer boutiques, see below), the experience could yield some useful shoes, black trousers, an odd tweed or satin jacket, maybe a coat and probably a bathing suit. Do not expect to see that classic you craved. You cannot ask the sales staff to put items on hold for you (they won't do it unless you are famous), so if you find a treasure, buy it on the spot. It will not stay long on the rack. Chanel, for one, does not send leftover things to the grey market in eastern Europe, who are now free and rich and buying here. The dross goes into a shredder, most likely, or might end up in a discount shopping mall in the suburbs of Nice.

The Chic Boutique Sales
There are many designer shops that offer good opportunities for the dis-

cerning shopper. Check the post for invitations and get on the mailing lists of shops you like. Leave your phone number with a sales assistant who can take a note of your requirements and telephone you if and when the piece is reduced in price. Watch the windows for sale signs, and get there early if you can; otherwise your size will be gone.

The most practical things to search for are the classics: the well-cut and non-seasonal pieces. One exception to this rule is to buy that strangely interesting thing you saw and craved a few months ago but is now hugely reduced (maybe no one else looked as good in it as you do – you always had a thing for bat-winged, shredded sleeves). At less than half the price, you can afford to have some fun and take risks.

Speciality shops, such as those that sell cashmere, are worth a visit, but again, you may be frustrated that the lovely colours are all gone, and you will be confronted with the new season's stuff (naturally unavailable at reduced prices). The sales are designed to clean out the dregs and, more importantly, to whet your appetite for the new collection, which happens to be sitting right there, larger than life, next to all the old, tired things.

Coats
These are the best things to buy at sales. They hardly ever go out of fashion, unless there is a radical change in shoulders. At the end of the selling season, which, incidentally, is right in the middle of the season when you wear them, go out and look for a good camel hair or navy cashmere coat. Loro Piana always seems to have a sales selection of fur-collared storm jackets and belted coats in larger sizes. You might find the trench coat of the year at Prada or Burberry. If you see something in leather in your size, or even the next size up, grab it. Leather is expensive, goes everywhere, hardly ever changes in style and looks good slightly bigger (but avoid trousers if they are too large as they will only stretch and become shapeless). Look out for bomber jackets and blazers.

If a shop specializes in classic trousers and jackets, such as hunting, fishing and shooting clothes, jump on your bike and get there early. You can find great buys at Holland and Holland, Purdey and Farlow. Their stock is this season's, and your current wardrobe will be much refreshed.

Post-Christmas sales are the most frustrating. You may stumble across that piece you had just bought at full price, which now, in the sale, is priced at a third off. Ignore the feeling of betrayal and move on. If you had waited, it probably would not have been there in your size.

Shoes
Specialist shoe shops at the top end of the market, such as Christian

Louboutin, Fratelli Rossetti and Tod's, sell off their stock at the end of the season. They do not normally load up on mistakes that no one wants. You would do well to go on the first or last day of the sale. On the first, you will certainly find your right size; on the last, they will probably reduce everything further.

Sales Rules

When buying clothes, only purchase a larger or smaller size than you usually wear if the shop will do the alterations for you. You will probably be charged for this, but at least the alterations person will understand the cut and finish of the piece, unlike the tailor at your local dry-cleaner's, who may not have the skills or knowledge to adjust the item correctly. Never buy anything with damage or a stain, even if the shop assistant swears up and down that it can be repaired or cleaned. Insist they clean it, with the proviso that if it is not perfect you will get your money back.

Never buy something because you see another woman trying it on, and it is not something you would normally wear. What looks good on her may be a travesty on you. Do not go to the sales with your best friend. You will either pass things up because she does not like them, or concentrate far too much on her needs. ALWAYS GO ALONE to preserve your sanity (and to hide your selfish instincts from those who know you – sales are war zones, and competition with your friends is ugly).

More mistakes are made at the sales than at any other time. The experience is fast, pressured, and the thought of saving money can make you irrational. Take stock, and take your time. Resist the ultra-high-fashion thing if you can, as it will probably lose its fascination as soon as the season ends. Sales of panty hose are the best. That is where you can find the real bargains.

Trunk Shows

Trunk shows have been around forever and seem to be an increasingly popular way of presenting a new collection. Here is how they work. If you are a regular and even not-so-regular customer of a shop (no matter that you only once bought a wallet), you are on their list. Well before pieces hit the ground, you will receive an invitation to an early and exclusive viewing of the coming season's collection. On the hottest day of the year, in the middle of June, you will be asked to preview winter clothes. This is of course absurd, but *go*. They may telephone you and offer a viewing time to suit. You may see the collection on video, glance through a so-called 'look book' or see the pieces on live models. Breakfast may be offered, or at the very least a coffee, glass of champagne or a canapé or two. The sample collection will probably be on hangers, and if you are the right size, close enough, this is an opportunity to try on pieces. Sales staff will demonstrate how the clothes should be worn. Their objective is to get you to order your choice in advance, one or two pieces at least, and sometimes there is some pressure to do so. If you are happy to order ahead, some shops may ask for a deposit. Only give your credit card as a deposit if you have fallen in love. Other stores will simply suggest that when the item arrives they will call you to try it on, without obligation. It will have your name on it, but there is a time limit. If you do not answer the telephone, overnight the piece will disappear to the next lucky customer down the waiting list. There is always the possibility that this coveted treasure may end up without a buyer, but in that case you will probably meet it again in the sales.

This is a civilized way to view new collections, get the jump on everyone else and to know the sales staff better. A *vendeuse* who keeps you in mind is worth her weight in truffles. A friendly greeting in a shop, even when you are just browsing, is a mood enhancer. If you see nothing you like, or are not quite sure how a piece will look in your proper size or how the item will fit into your existing wardrobe, then the experience might seem a bit intimidating.

We advise you to take a deep breath, keep smiling, enjoy the half-hour and gently say you will think about it. Sales managers give mixed reports of the usefulness of trunk shows and are unsure how their customers will react. Some clients appear to like the experience and others not. Do not go if you are uncomfortable with the idea of having to make decisions so far in advance of the next season. As with everything in the fashion world, trunk shows seem so out of sync. You have only just managed to buy a couple of pairs of shorts and a bathing suit for the summer, when you are bombarded with invitations to choose your winter wardrobe. It is worth bearing in mind that you will have the first choice of the best in the collection, in your size, with no worries.

There are fundamental economic reasons why trunk shows are used more and more as a marketing device. The store is assured of a certain number of pre-sales. They need not order much more than they can initially sell. This means less overstock and fewer losers that have to be disposed at sales. The trunk show also functions as market research. Designers usually present large collections on the catwalks, which individual store buyers edit for their own customers. A trunk show can provide a good forecast that a particular item from the collection will prove popular, which a buyer can then order in several sizes, while other pieces will be rejected in their entirety. There have always been trunk shows in the United States. Designers took their collections to major cities to show them to their coteries of admirers. Legendary Bill Blass was a prime example. He was charming, handsome and witty and always brought wonderful, grown-up 'lux' clothes – his trunk shows were sell-outs.

Today, the designer does not travel with his "trunk," but sales staff know how the clothes should be worn and with what accessories. It is important to learn how to coordinate a new idea and that's why a glance at the 'look book' or video will show you how it is done. But don't forget the other designers that you admire and how your purchases from each will go together. Can you wear that Anne Demeulemeester cardigan with the triple zippers with that op-art skirt by Diane von Furstenberg?

Most designers also have a preview day when you can pop in and look at the new season's offerings. But remember that once the season gets started, the women who ordered initially at the trunk shows are the ones who will receive preferential treatment. If you work and have little free time, preview days can be great time-savers. You can order your requests by telephone at a later time (having already tried them on), eliminating the need for you to return to the shop in person.

There are other kinds of trunk shows. You might be asked to view the collection of an unknown designer at someone's home, or at a hotel. Some shows focus on "discounted" lines, which can be viewed over one or two days in a specially rented space. These types of show happen quite a bit in London these days, especially around Christmas, and you can find all kinds of bags, scarves, jewellery and clothes to give away as gifts (these accessories may be handy for all the carol services and mulled-wine parties you will be attending). Trunk shows for charity are also popular, but it may be difficult to escape without buying something small (for a good cause).

Travelling jewellers, especially those at the top end of the market, also hold trunk shows. We find that these can be the most pressuring experiences of all. Viewings always seem to take place in very small, personal spaces where you are greeted at the door, possibly by the designer. There is a limited-time element, and a lot of cooing and air-kissing between previous customers and staff. There will be pressure to try things on, and the prices are not always obvious. You will be forced to ask the cost, usually of a girl half your age, bedecked in jewels she could never afford herself. The answer is usually "a very affordable £15,000." The graceful way to decline, while avoiding any self-consciousness or reluctance to commit, is merely to ask the assistant to write down the details on the store's business card and tell her that you will contact the main branch when you are next visiting. If all else fails, just say how lovely the pieces are and leave.

The trunk show demonstrates the true power of salesmanship and, as such, can be an interesting experience. You will be treated royally, shown exclusive things, possibly offered alcohol and other treats and be showered with compliments about "how wonderful madam looks." But do not fall for it and do not make your mind up at a sprinter's pace. If in doubt, limit yourself to one glass of champagne and control that urge to become the new Mrs Trump look-alike.

CHAPTER TWENTY-SEVEN

The Language of Luxury

I t never fails to entertain us that there is an industry in "luxury." After all, luxury connotes limited supply and uncompromising standards. How on earth can an *industry* supply an unlimited number of so-called exclusive goods? Is Louis Vuitton a luxury manufacturer? For many, the brand is a cult, a fashion statement, something utilitarian, a status symbol, a desperate kind of trendiness – but a *luxury*? Can you buy luxury at the Duty Free? Does luxury have a timeless quality, or is it subject to the shifting vagaries of supply and demand in the fashion business? The answer is a qualified "yes" to all of the above.

If one were to describe luxury for the grown-up woman, it could be seen as a temptation and as an exquisite fulfilment, the distillation of visual and tactile pleasure. It is not fashion, but it can set trends. Luxury is knowledge and experience. In order to understand this, you must have some basis of comparison.

We may not as a rule display our silk bra and panties with hand-embroidered butterflies, but we know we are wearing them. There is a kind of secret intimacy about true luxury. We turn our beautiful emerald solitaire inward when we are on the street, or cover it with gloves, but it is there on our finger, and we know it. We wear fur on the inside of a coat, or trimmed discreetly on the collar of a designer suit. We buy a beautifully tailored blonde cashmere coat or jacket, and we revel in its softness and warmth; it need not have any labels or logos on it. It makes us feel better.

Luxury is snobbish. Luxury is selfish. It is the polar opposite of democracy. It does not share well unless it is a half-pound of Beluga. It is freedom to buy something unique and special, which has nothing to do with another person's well-being. You select it because you can afford it, have saved for it, maybe sacrificed for it. Sometimes it is a gift to yourself, and sometimes it is a special expression of love and value from someone else.

Luxury is care, maintenance. If something is a luxury, it cannot – and should not – be treated harshly. There is nothing more irritating than seeing a woman carrying a Hermès bag in a careless or disrespectful way. This is a mindless lack of appreciation and arrogance that has nothing to do with luxury.

Luxury is limited. It is not about waiting lists, though it can be. Luxury is something you discover, that few others know about (and if they do, they are discreet). They might share this secret source with a good friend, but maybe not. Luxury is about the beautiful and sensual. Luxury is seductive. It calls to your deepest feelings in some fundamental way. It speaks the universal language of desire. Luxury is something that ultimately satisfies – aesthetically, sensually and even intellectually.

What are Luxury Items?
Hand-made, with the utmost care to detail, subtle, sophisticated, perhaps soft to the touch, light, flexible, full of integrity, charm and elegance. Luxury has the most style because it is timeless. What could be more luxurious than a soft-as-butter, creamy golden, woven leather or cognac-coloured crocodile bag? Does it matter that it comes from Bottega Veneta or Hermès, or a tiny specialist shop that you stumbled across in Florence or Tunbridge Wells? Is there anything more special than a swansdown, soft suede jacket in the most fragile shade of pink? Or a pair of Nile-green lambskin gloves from the Rue de Rivoli? Coco Chanel said that luxury was the only necessity, and we all know that she was right.

Cashmere
There are probably more grades of cashmere than any of us can name, but the finest producers weave and knit from a grade that is distinguished by its feel, the way the dye takes, the way it drapes and ultimately its price. The finest luxurious cashmere is never cheap. The quality you find in the High Street or at Gap (no offense intended) is simply not luxury. If you want a piece of luxury cashmere, the measurement is always touch. Many good manufacturers today control supplies to ensure that there is consistency in their production.

Traditional high-quality producers, such as Pringle of Scotland, have improved their designs exponentially so that you do not have to sacrifice style for quality. Having married luxury with fashion, they have moved beyond boxy, boring twin-sets. Fine cashmere leggings are great for overnight flights, as are pashminas. Visit Loro Piana just to smooth your hands over one of their cashmere shawls edged with chinchilla. Swoon a little.

Silk

When it is good quality – heavy in weight, cut well and made into objects of desire, whether lingerie, dresses, blouses or scarves – silk is a luxury item. It is not when it is heavily dyed and stiff, badly cut, flimsy, easily torn and sold by the kilo. In today's fashion world, silk is distressed, ruched, bunched, cut, shrunk and manipulated. Woven, knitted and blended, it can be commonplace and ubiquitous. Silk has the singular advantage of being warm when it is cold, and cool when it is hot. It is a natural air-conditioner and does well in any climate, depending on its weight. A Prada silk chiffon blouse with delicate tucks and stitching worn under a tailored suit is a luxury item. A hand-made silk nightie with fine lace trim is a luxury. Hand-embroidered silk is a luxury. There is a lot of silk about, but most of it is High Street production – stylish and fun, but only the finest quality can be said to be luxury.

Linen

Romantic and with a status all its own, linen's appeal goes beyond price. We call it a luxury when used in bed sheets because you need a good laundress to care for it. In clothing, it is a luxurious necessity. The most obvious characteristic of good linen is that when it wrinkles (which all linens do), it wrinkles beautifully in long, loose lines and rumples in an elegant, Edwardian kind of way. Imagine the Raj.

Linen dyes beautifully and is most luxurious in natural tones: off-white, saffron, beige, honey, taupe, pale-green, milk-chocolate and toffee. It looks good in black or dead-white and cheesy in bright, artificial shades. Leave the bright-pinks, neon-reds, electric-blues and sunflower-yellows to cotton, which takes strong colour better and has a crispness that complements sharper tones. Linen looks good loose, and is most luxurious in drawstring trousers and cargo pants, well-cut shirts, blouses, burnooses and caftans.

Good linen is expensive but lasts forever. The more it is washed, the more beautiful it becomes. A linen handkerchief, trimmed in lace or hand-embroidered with your initials, is a thing to behold – luxurious and beautiful.

Cotton

You could say that cotton is cheap and cheerful and not a luxury at all.

What we see in the High Street shops are less expensive grades and blends. You must seek out truly luxurious cottons in speciality shops and brands. The difference between a well-cut, Sea Island cotton shirt and an off-the-peg model in a mass-market shop is amazing. The luxurious cotton dress, blouse, sweater or trouser is fine to the touch, heavy of hand, smooth as butter and, whether close or loosely woven, has a shape that keeps through endless washings. It cuts and takes detail well, looks sharp and crisp, and is hugely adaptable. What could be more useful, smart and sexy than a beautiful, white cotton man-tailored shirt?

Cotton is a fabric for all seasons, especially spring and summer. Look for a pique cotton shift dress or a heavy navy-blue jacket to wear with white jeans. Cotton makes great trousers, jeans, jackets, T-shirts, skirts and sweaters. It travels well. Cotton can be woven in myriad ways, from the gauziest see-through organdies and voiles to heavy satins and nubby tweeds. Judge it by feel. Pure cotton will feel cool to the hand compared to cotton-blends, which always feel a bit tacky. Add a tiny percentage of lycra to cotton and you have a crisp look with a bit of stretch that will, when washed, rebound to its original shape. Be prepared to pay for the best, knowing that it will last.

Fur

Fur is controversial in some places. In the U.K. and U.S.A., your attitude towards fur puts you in one moral camp or the other. The anti-fur movement has some kinship with environmentalism. If you do not wear fur, you will probably not wear leather. Stella McCartney caters to customers who prefer not to do either. Outside the Anglo-American sphere, however, not everyone agrees about the fur issue. European women, for example, seem unconcerned. Unless you are seriously committed to moral ideas against eating or using animal by-products, fur has a neutral quality, like buying chicken at the supermarket. We believe that animals for food and clothing should be raised with consideration for their care and comfort, and that they should be killed humanely. Cruelty to any living thing is unacceptable.

Fur is a definite luxury. It is beautiful, both lightweight and warm – warmer in fact than any fabric other than a silver-foiled rescue cloak. It makes an unequalled coat, jacket or lining, and in a cold climate there is nothing to compare. Sable is the ultimate fur. Rabbit is not. Mink comes in a thousand mutations or shades and is bred for multiple use; the most beautiful variety is the so-called "wild mink." Not in fact feral, they are a species originally taken from the countryside and farmed. The best and most luxurious minks are developed for their lightness and warmth; the female skins are the silkiest and most desirable.

Today, mink is woven, shredded, mixed with silk or leather, scraped, clipped, trimmed and embroidered. There is nothing more practical or sexy. Our notions about fur might be atavistic, reaching back to our distant origins on the tundra. We still respond emotionally to its sensual colours and feel – no amount of anti-hype can deny our attraction to it. You, however, must make up your own mind. If you want to explore, J. Mendel and Dennis Basso in New York City are the ultimate purveyors of the moment. Mendel's windows are especially seductive, one day showing a full-length chinchilla coat, the next a shell pink mink capelet over a satin, bias-cut evening gown dyed the same blushing shade. This is serious temptation and one of the ultimate luxuries.

Innovations

Every so often, scientists develop something in the laboratories that falls under the category of luxury. Ultra-suede, in the 1970s, was such an item. It looked like suede but washed like rubber. Everyone wanted it for suits and trousers. It was a luxury fashion item and very expensive. As it began to be imitated and produced more plentifully, however, it became cheaper and lost its cachet. Today, you can buy it as expensive upholstery material, but it is no longer used for luxury clothes.

Microfibres were developed in the 1980s. Revolutionary for their warmth, lightness and smoothness to the touch, they made incredibly expensive and effective rainwear. Today, they are commonplace and found in all manner of sports and all-weather clothes – available as fishing, hunting and climbing gear, ski clothes, leisure suits and running shorts. They have passed into ordinary use and lost their status.

Today, nylon is the ultimate in common usage and common sense. There is a strange irony that something discovered during the Second World War, when silk was unavailable for stockings, and has been cheap and ever-present since, should now be considered a luxury material. Prada made it so. As a big, chic black Prada satchel, nylon is considered both elitist and utilitarian. As Tumi and Brics luggage, it is indestructible, easy to clean, impervious to the harms of travel, very expensive and therefore a luxury.

A number of designers, notably Issey Miyake and Jil Sander, have always played with innovative fabrics and created new concepts for the luxury fashion market. Miyake, for example, produced a treated, woven cotton that stretched like wool, but maintained its innate lightness and comfort. Make a point, however, of reading the care labels of the newer, blended fabrics, as several are not happy in the rain, or require special treatment.

Time

Time is the ultimate luxury. We cannot buy it, but we can make it. The ageing process is time passing. It can mean giving up and giving in. It can mean letting the weight pile on and the muscles sag. It can mean depression and loss of self-confidence. It can also signal new beginnings and a fresh assessment of your potential. It can mean letting go of previous responsibilities that are no longer relevant. Fashion and a brave new look can be one very important and satisfying interest, even if you never had it before. Make some time for it.

PLEASURE
AND
LEISURE

CHAPTER TWENTY-EIGHT

Exercise Gear

Not all of us wants to exercise, to keep our connective tissues connected, our bones protected and our energy levels rejuvenated, but it is a well-known fact that only exercise can provide this, so start moving. If weights leave you cold, and yoga is too boring, there are always games like tennis and golf. For these sports, there is a broad range of exercise gear that will suit your sense of play.

Golf

There is not a lot you can do to make yourself look fit and attractive on the course. Dressing for golf is a question of common practice, dress codes and club rules. Women look better when their outfits fit properly, but for golf, looseness and comfort is important to the swing, thus fabrics with lycra are a real bonus. As you are essentially on an extended walk, dress in layers to accommodate that cold gust of wind, blinding bit of hot sun or sudden rain storm, conditions players in Ireland and Scotland know well. Everything can fit into your Yonex golf club bag. A divided skirt could look retro and cute with a fitted, short-sleeved knitted shirt and contrasting v-neck cardigan. Keep socks short to show your ankles. Trousers should fit well across the buttocks and hips, with pleats in the front and a slightly low rise to accommodate movement. We like the look of a trim navy-blue polo shirt, navy trousers with no belt (for once), a white cable knit cardigan and a little red neckerchief. Conversely, grey-, beige- and peach-coloured clothes with tan golf shoes also look very smart. Black only ever looked good on the South African golfer,

Gary Player. Bermuda shorts are for high summer – slightly flared, in pretty pastels with matching shirts and socks.

It's important to be light and bright since you are out on a green and beige landscape. You need to be seen to avoid accidents. You do not need to look masculine, unless you want to. You can always add a pretty detail that keeps you looking chic and appropriate at the same time. Try small earrings and a sports watch.

Tennis

Racquet sports have their own dress codes. Tennis clothes should be well tailored and emphasize your good features – legs, arms, shoulders – and allow freedom of movement. Buy yourself new outfits every season to avoid that rumpled "I don't care about myself look," and make sure they are washed well, especially if you play on red clay. Buy a comfortable, supportive sports bra. You do not want to be pulling and tugging at it after every stroke. Support, not lift and separate, as exercise guru Frank Shipman says, unless you want two black eyes. As varicose veins are off-putting, try applying a St Tropez tan at the start of the season, especially if you plan to be in shorts or a short skirt. And retire that old, used tennis dress or misshapen pair of shorts and get something new and useful.

White is best. Pastels could work, but some clubs may refuse you; dark colours make you look like you have a Boris Becker fetish (nothing wrong with that). The combination of a light top and dark bottoms is a kind of girl guides look. Why not?

We buy shorts and T-shirts at Gap, or Ralph Lauren when we are feeling rich. Shorts should be somewhere between mid-thigh, slightly flared and made of natural materials, such as cotton and linen, so your skin can breathe. The mid-thigh cut avoids that one area of flab that, sadly, we all have, and should sit slightly off the waist for comfort and to give the appearance of a longer waist. Add a tiny string of pearls or a small shell necklace for a bit of style. The boyish, man-tailored look, as long as it is not too butch, also has charm, and the sharp cut and clean lines will make your figure look and feel better. We do not like artificial fabrics that look like food wrapping and usually come in harsh colours with stripes and slashes, rips and hanging threads. These trendy but trashy items will be out of style in a minute. Avoid bicycling shorts like malaria.

Every outfit should have pockets. Nothing is worse than having to stuff a tennis ball or three up your underpants. Avoid logos blazoned across your chest or back, although a brand name of some kind or other is bound to be somewhere on the garment. Keep it discreet if you can.

Keep a pretty cashmere or cotton cardigan handy to throw over your shoulders or tie around your waist in case you get chilly when the sun goes down. Absolutely forget the man-tailored blue blazer but do consider a cute, cotton bomber jacket to wear over your shorts. Take a canvas satchel, a bottle of water, sunscreen SPF15, a small towel and Jurlique rosewater spray to freshen up.

Skiing

Some of us consider that, post-youth, skiing is an extreme form of sado-masochism, designed to form little broken blood vessels in your cheeks, break your bones and wrench your back. But many of us still love it, and for you, there are wonderful sports departments everywhere to meet your needs.

The same rules apply to ski clothes as to other kinds of sportswear: minimize your bad features and maximize the good. Padded clothes, for example, will increase your girth, but you can console yourself because few people, save models, look good in them. Sleeker, darker "miracle" materials suit most of us better. One piece salopettes are a misery to get out of, especially at lunch time when you need the loo. Who cannot fail to remember that moment of fear when the top end grazes or actually falls into the toilet as you gracefully prepare to sit down? If you seek to reduce the appearance of your size, always stick to the one-colour rule. White ski-suits with splashes of colour are glamourous, but there are far too many snowboarders and extreme sports teenagers out there, and it is vital that you are seen from afar to avoid injury. One friend of ours was broadsided by an unguided fourteen-year-old missile in Gstaad, and had to be airlifted out to sew her face back on. She was wearing white. Stick to strong solid colours on the slopes.

Remember to bring a fabulous pair of dark sunglasses. You need them for glare, and they reek of glamour (see chapter on sunglasses), but try not to fall on your face while wearing them. Sports stores try to sell us goggles, but we find these impractical as they mist up and you cannot see a thing. We also love furry ski hats, for skiing or not. Stay away from balaclavas unless you plan to rob a bank.

Après-ski is another serious aspect of alpine holidays. Know your location, and discuss the mode of dress with either your travel agent, the hotel concierge or look it up on the Web. Resorts vary enormously, country to country, inexpensive to big time. If you are still skiing after all these years, you are probably going to resorts that you know already and love. Still, it is fun to buy a couple of new gorgeous things – for example, a pair of smart black trousers with a beautiful cashmere, beaded sweater in a jewel-like colour. If it is a low-key, low-profile, hang-loose kind of resort, your good parka and some great weather boots will be casually chic. If it is Aspen, St Moritz, Gstaad or Vail, raise the fashion ante at night and wear a smart jacket with a printed shawl and good jewellery. Bring a fur-lined trimmed parka and, if you have one, a fur coat – the bigger and fuzzier the better; for these occasions, gargantuan is good.

Wear layers because everyone keeps their chalets hot these days. In Austria and Switzerland, it is chic to do Tyrolean style with grey, boiled-wool jackets trimmed in green, red and silver; forget the dirndls. In many resorts, you can find after-ski clothes right at your doorstep. Aspen is serious shopping, where you can find every brand of sportswear, not to mention jewellery and fashionable city clothes. Don't leave too much for the trip, however, as the hardest thing to get your hands on will be ski clothes in your size, so it's best to bring your own.

Outdoor and Indoor Activities

Power-walking, jogging, rollerblading and bicycling all require protective outdoor clothing. What you wear will depend largely on the weather, even the traffic. Bright colours are a service to yourself and others at dawn and twilight for visibility. Knee and elbow padding may be required for skating and bicycling, especially if your balance is a bit off.

Whether you go to a gym or exercise at home, the question about what to wear inside is just the same – lycra or not? Short or long, tight or loose, cotton or techno-fibre? Black, white or coloured; inner bra, support bra, no bra; thong, bikini pants, no pants? Modesty or let it all hang out? Although exercise might be something you do basically for yourself, you still need to worry about what you look like. After all, you may be walking to the gym, and you never know who you might run into. When we do yoga, pilates, aerobics, cross-training, running for a marathon or just getting fit before a ski trip or a favourite cocktail dress, we are still ourselves. We want to look good, even if it is only for that person staring back at you in the treadmill mirror. Floppy old track-suits and a worn, stained singlet will not reinforce our self-esteem, regardless of the context. We need comfort *and* style, support, temperature control, fabric breathability and a bit of sex appeal. We love lycra for working out. It makes you feel taut and young, but too much of it and you will burn up. Always check labels carefully for the percentage of lycra versus natural fabrics.

You can always find exercise clothes in department stores and sporting shops, but our favourite haunts are in hotel spas. American brands made of cotton, with a touch of lycra, are usually inexpensive, last through a hundred washings and are young and cute. Look for yoga pants that are a bit looser than leggings, and tops with built-in bras (for headstands). Pieces by Nike are good because they wash well and dry quickly, but they can appear rather plastic and come in some unflattering colours. We prefer something more feminine and personal. By the way, do wear lipstick when you work out – it helps you to look more alive through your kick-boxing sessions. Some women like everything sleeveless because they feel less constricted, but if you do not like your upper arms, go for the cap-sleeve. Do not wear anything long-sleeved unless you are running outside in arctic temperatures. For this climate, the classic black or navy-blue track-suit with a woolly hat and scarf is de rigueur. A little pair of star-stud earrings and a plastic watch will take you to Starbucks afterwards.

No-Nos

No bicycling shorts with long loose T-shirts after fifty. You hate your upper body and love your legs, but consider this: the bulky shirt hides the truth from you and no one else, and gets in the way of useful movement. Bicycling shorts, which show a mature woman's body in the most unattractive way, are for the Tour de France team and young roller-bladers. They should only be worn in utter desperation in the privacy of your own home, if you have run out of alternatives. Very loose knitted shorts with wide legs can be most immodest when you are crossing and uncrossing your legs or when exercising and stretching. Better to buy below-the-knee-length drawstring trousers. They are cool in every sense and practical.

On the subject of shell suits. If you still have a nylon one, give it away now to your favourite charity. Tight towelling suits may have been yesterday's must-have, but even on an eighteen-year-old they were deadly. They emphasized every bulge, every wayward curve, made a woman look cheap and, worse, lazy. Why would anyone think that these sartorial attacks on your self-esteem were attractive? It is better to buy a grey work-out outfit to go with your trainers than a hyped-up suit emblazoned with PERFECT across the bottom. In London, good tracksuits can be found at Sweaty Betty chain shops, and the Kings Road Sports Shop. If you have a great desire to dress down (see below) and are extremely rich, you can do it elegantly with a lightweight, cashmere tracksuit from Loro Piana in grey, navy-blue or black. If your work-out space is freezing cold, try long (preferably silk) underwear. It is warm and keeps your body temperature at a constant level.

Dressing Down

The concept of dressing down has infected the world like avian flu. We understand it to be a more democratic form of dress that says, as jeans once did: "We are all the same. I am not pulling rank on you in my haute couture. I am savvy, hip, cool and have street-cred." We are all prone to these trends, but like everything else that says uniformity, we want to rebel against the rebellion. Our daughters wore school uniforms and either hiked them up or pulled them down; sometimes they shredded them or added strange tribal details. On the one hand we want to be low on the horizon line, in sync with the rest of humanity, but at the same time we shout in agony at being anonymous and invisible. Hence, if we can afford it, we seek out the most expensive form of the same thing that everyone else is wearing.

In the realm of dressing down, concentrate on buying things that are good quality but not extravagant. If you like wearing track-suits, opt for classic styles and colours. Keep them clean and replace them when they get worn. Carry a smart, sporty handbag and wear a crisp new pair of trainers – save your real money for real clothes. But do not spend all of your time in comfortable, exercise regalia. You are certain to gain a lot of weight without noticing (elasticated waists will stretch out with you) unless you are on a body-building mission to look like Bridget Jones.

CHAPTER TWENTY-NINE

What to Wear by the Sea

s the body ages, the bathing suit presents a number of problems, principally its tendency to fall south. It would be a bit much to wear lycra pantyhose under a one-piece swimsuit, as we once witnessed in the south of France on a middle-aged woman who seemed to be recovering from extensive, head-to-toe plastic surgery. She claimed the hose kept her flesh from sliding, but needless to say, this was not a good look.

Barring such extreme measures, it is inevitable that at fifty-plus we are not the same as we were at thirty or forty. We may be fit and strong, and many of us can look less than our real age – toned, tanned and pretty decent in our normal clothes – but the bathing suit is a real test of confidence. The skin is more slack, and its texture has perhaps roughened a bit. There are veins and some spotty brown flaws. The space between the thighs has either bowed out or filled in.

The body beautiful that might have once been your pride and joy at the beach, certain to get admiring glances, has become just another collection of flesh and bones and is no longer pulling the right attention. Do not despair. From here on out, everything will become attitude and mystery.

We may no longer be pulchritudinous perfection, but we are still women. And in our maturity we have the ability to surround ourselves in mystery. One way we can do this is through how much we reveal. If you are so out of shape that you feel you must not show your flesh, you may be right. Now might be the time to invest in some elegant, loose-

s the body ages, the bathing suit presents a number of problems, linen drawstring trousers, a gauzy top, a large straw hat, big sunglasses and to lounge languorously under an umbrella. Wear bright lipstick, read a good book and take a sketch pad.

If, however, you think your shape is still good enough, here are some thoughts. Before you go on a sun-filled holiday, have some St Tropez or other good brand of fake tan applied, preferably at a reputable local beauty salon. There are many at-home products, but, alas, most make you look a bit jaundiced. The point of St Tropez or "fantasy tan" is to have a light bronzing on your body and face for the beginning of the holiday, so that tiny veins and imperfections are concealed by a golden glow. Do not forget your suntan lotion as the fake tan does not protect you from the harmful rays of the sun.

Buy a new swimming costume because last year's model will have deteriorated from chlorine, multiple washings and sun. The elastic will be looser and leave unattractive gaps. The bathing suit ages faster than we do, so turf out all your old suits, no matter how much you love them. Go to a good department store or speciality shop and try on an assortment, which, it is true, can be a trauma. The dressing room is probably small and cramped, and, worse still, you may have to go out into the corridor to see yourself in a larger mirror. Wear tiny panties, and take off your panty hose, which might be a struggle and would snag, but in the end it will be worth the effort. In the dressing room, look at yourself close up and check every part of your body: breasts, back, sides and underarms. Examine your legs, thighs and the backs of your knees. In the three-way mirrors you will see the bad and the good, but you do not have to be perfect. As you try on each suit, check the fit, the length and support. Look for comfort. If it is sliding upwards or down, does something need adjusting? If not, forget this item because it won't get any better in the pool. Bathing suits are very body specific and one cut may do wonders, whilst another will completely destroy your self-esteem. If you are too shy to show the saleswomen how you look, you will never make it onto the beach! Check to see if the suit comes with a matching cover-up if you feel at all embarrassed. This might improve the look enormously.

The Anglo-American designer Liza Bruce makes terrific swimsuits, with a cut that is never too demanding. Her designs lengthen the leg with high, cut-away thighs without being immodest. Their shape and snug fit, made of springy, heavy-gauge nylon, make your body appear smoother and more sculpted. Erès and La Perla are the Rolls Royce of swimwear. Their designs suit all kinds of bodies thanks to their cut and support, and can be found as bikinis and one-pieces (maillots). Calvin Klein and Jantzen make great, sporty one-piece suits intended for serious swimming, some with construction within, some without. With its comprehensive approach to figure flaws, midriff bloat, derrière spread and general flab, Gottex is the middle-aged woman's alternative to Prozac and the biggest sellers in any bathing-suit department for the grown-up set.

We all have favourite colours. Surprisingly, white can be flattering, with bikinis and one-piece looking as good on pale skin as on dark. There's a summer sexiness to them, without being too overt. Most good-quality white swimsuits have a flesh-coloured inner lining, but there is still a hint of transparency. We love white because it is clean-looking and sharp. It says fresh air, bracing waves and is perennially classic. Be careful when applying sun creams and oils, however, to avoid stains.

We love aquamarine, Gitane-blue, lime, lavender, rose, chartreuse and tangerine. These are hot-weather colours full of sunny vitality. They look good with tanned skin, real or fake. We strongly advise that you wean yourself off black, once and for all. On the younger you, black swimsuits were sleek and panther-like. You might have worn very tiny bikinis or low-cut maillots. But by now, have you considered how dull they can be? You may think that you are hiding deficiencies under that solid black number, but we think that the darkness draws attention to body flaws. The more there is of this heavy blackness, the sadder you look. So free yourself of the delusion that black suits will minimize and flatter. They are just no fun.

A printed bathing suit can be pretty, feminine and a good disguise for body imperfections because it draws the eye away from pure outline. Pucci prints and polka-dots are cute and perky, and flowers can be sweet – especially on a well-cut suit. Stripes are demanding no matter which way they run.

Should you wear one piece or two? A bikini is fine at any age on a private boat, by the beach and on a lounge chair. If your body is trim and muscular they are wonderful because they are lightweight, comfortable and dry in a minute. It does not matter that your tummy may be less taut than a washboard, as long as you are reasonably tan. But in a more crowded and hence more intimate setting, such as by a hotel or club pool (where through sheer boredom everyone is watching every curve, line and flaw), avoid anything that will cause you to be insecure. Highly stylized two-piece bathing suits that do not fall into the bikini category belong only on tall, straight, small-breasted bodies with long legs. Bikinis give the effect of longer length between the bra and the pants, and lend themselves to all types of attractive cover-ups. Tie a pareu around your bosom, or wear harem or cargo pants, shorts, a caftan, see-through sarong or an amusing ankle-length T-shirt. Do not tie a sarong around your lower hips unless you are slim, as it will only emphasize a slack waist and heavier hips.

At our age, you also need to think about what the swimsuit is *not* covering. Nothing is more ageing than skin that has absorbed a full blast of rays. Protect yourself always with cream and an umbrella. When buying a new suit, buy a cut that accommodates your bottom in an attractive way – in other words, cover the crease. Look at the upper thighs and crotch: suits cut too high on the leg are unflattering as our skin becomes more crinkly. Consider your bosom – do you want to reveal your breasts? Uplift is the paramount consideration. Avoid suits that make you appear as if you have two solid grapefruits on your chest, or ones that flatten you like a gigantic, crêpe suzette. The strapless bandeau is a particular culprit, widening and flattening everyone (and making flesh pop out in all the wrong places). Heart-shaped necks give a nice indication of cleavage without showing too much. Straight-across cuts with wide straps look youthful and chic, but stay away from plunging necklines as they can be unnerving for others. They only look good on the very young, if at all.

Backless bathing suits are difficult to wear unless you have a taut, smooth, blemish-free back. Cut-outs are tricky because they can make your flesh peer out in all sorts of odd places and may cause you to tan in patterns (though you are not meant to be in the sun). These require the kind of solid flesh that most of us have no longer. Still, a subtle little slash here and there never did anyone any harm.

Today's miracle fibres have done wonders for the bathing suit. They cling and control, which is good if you are feeling a bit overfed. Too much cling, however, is not attractive, and you should avoid suits that are too tight or made of heavy fabric, which will render you paralytic with discomfort (and never dry).

Leopards, Tigers, Zebras: The Tarzan-Meets-Jane Look

Everyone seems to have an opinion on the jungle look. There was a time that the spotted animal print (à la Raquel Welch), with big hair, gold jewellery, huge hoop earrings and high-heeled mules, was sexy and chic on the beach. Of course, you had to be somewhere on the Mediterranean. It can work on the young, with their smooth skin and innocent, makeup-free faces. There is, after all, something very erotic about animal skins and their replicas. Sadly, though, it is not for us, even on the glitziest beach at St Tropez. Why, you might ask?

The answer is, to put it mildly, because they reek of the obvious, the inelegant, the crude, the rude and the bad. We are not prudes (nor do we want to destroy your fun), but this is a FACT. The same goes for diamanté, metallic studs, buckles, glittering lurex, silver sequins and platinum baubles tied onto shoe-lace straps. No, a thousand times NO. If you must have something dazzling, try just a touch of a gold line on an edge or strap, or a tiny, discreetly placed Swarovski crystal motif.

We love that some French and Italian women go topless, with tons of gold jewellery and gigantic white-rimmed sunglasses, because it is outrageous, but we won't go there. You have to be born to that look, it has to be in your cultural DNA. Mediterranean women seem to carry it off – to some extent. When a large-breasted northern European woman tries it, however, it is not the same thing. Her skin is wrong, her face and saucer-blue eyes are wrong, and her goose pimples are definitely wrong. So just wryly observe the look from afar, and don't even think about it.

Accessories

Along with your bathing suit, you will need a pretty straw or fabric beach bag, and some new flat clogs, slides or plastic flip-flops (with cherries on them) from Accessorize. Any heel higher than mid-height is trashy-looking. Good rules for hats: buy a big, simple straw hat in ivory, tobacco, cerise or any shade but black (which absorbs the sun's rays and will make you feel hot and exhausted) with quality and shape. Hats made by Caroline Charles, in straw or starched fabric, are pretty and good value. Forget about the cheap one you bought in the Caribbean last year as it is likely to have lost its appeal. If you like to wear jewellery, diamond ear-studs or thin gold hoops are good. Try a little ethnic or crystal bead necklace with a woven bracelet. No serious jewels, no tattoos, no henna designs.

Take an extra bathing suit to the pool or beach to change into from your soggy one later, along with such other necessities as one or two good books, sunglasses, creams, maybe a scarf to use as a bandana and a little eau de cologne for refreshment – Jo Malone's Fig and Nina Ricci's Belles de Ricci are light with citrus notes (see the chapter on Perfume).

No one wears rubber swimming caps anymore, but with the price of hair colouring being what it is, it's something we need to think about. If your hair is long, wear a hairband and tie it in a knot when you swim. Giant hair combs are good for this purpose. Your hair will stay out of the chlorinated water, and you will appear neater and more attractive without your locks flowing all around you. Besides, it is more hygienic and socially sensitive.

No mobile phones by the pool please. There is nothing more irritating or antisocial than having to listen to someone do business deals over their mobile (when you are all supposed to be resting). Keep yours switched off. Better still, leave it in your suitcase. Relax.

Sunglasses

Age defiance at the tip of your nose: the mature woman's best friend. They disguise wrinkles around the eyes, reduce squinting and protect against harmful UV rays. They give instant mystery, glamour and useful anonymity. If you are a person who craves privacy, then you *know* about sunglasses. Think Greta Garbo, Jackie O, Diane Keaton in wire-rimmed circles.

Almost all designers produce a line in sunglasses because, like handbags and shoes, it is a top money-spinner. New models seem to arrive in the shops every month, and just like the young, you can plug into the latest fashion immediately. Although you may have some fun with this, avoid certain styles. Pastel-tinted glasses in shades from rosy-pink to pale-yellow can give a dehydrated look to mature skin. Avoid metallic frames and mirrored lenses, which will do you no favours (unless you are being photographed for *Hello!* magazine). Keep away from large logos placed on the sides of the frame or on the central area, especially those of shiny metal and diamante. If you are not careful those upswept, gem-studded frames will make you look like Dame Edna, no matter how much you crave them. Likewise, discard those heavy squares of black plastic unless you want to be taken for Sergeant Bilko's daughter. Neither of these styles would be ironic on you.

We prefer classic shapes. They can be rectangular, circular or square, made of fake tortoiseshell or coloured plastic in neutral shades such as white, ivory, amber, grey, brown and black. We love punchy red, blue and purple frames, but only in reading glasses. If you are a bit into retro, try Ray Bans, which will help you drift into reveries about Steve McQueen. Lighter frames and paler colours are good for summer, although the classic black-framed Chanel prototype, with its very dark glass, can look incredibly chic at all times. They are great with jeans and surprisingly soothing to the eyes.

Try on several different styles to accommodate your mood swings, as well as your outfits. This can be frustrating in department stores, which often place security tags down the middle of the frames (in our experience, sale assistants are reluctant to remove them) or lock items behind metal bars. You might do better to visit your local optician's shop, which can be a treasure trove of the latest models.

Sunglasses are essential for power-walking because they protect your eyes from wind-blown grit and dust. An ophthalmologist will tell you that your retinas become increasingly vulnerable over time and should always be protected from the sun. Lightweight frames are best for comfort, and they will avoid putting pressure marks around your nose and cheeks (which, incidentally, can lead to an outbreak of little red veins). Avoid taking your best sunglasses to the beach, where they can get scratched by the sand or lost in the waves. If you prefer sunglasses that you can wear indoors as well as out, try prescription light-sensitive lenses that adjust automatically to the environment.

We probably all have collections of old, so-called 'vintage' sunglasses lying in the back of a drawer. They can be fun now and again, but it is better to forget about resurrecting what once was. Take a moment to reflect on the pair you wore in Amsterdam when you took a short course on Dutch flower painting, and then put them away. Console yourself with the fact that these days sunglasses are more comfortable and better engineered. Sunglasses are like perfume. They have attitude, but you can get bored of them. At the very least, have a few pairs handy for when a new mood strikes and stay up-to-date.

Resort Clothes

Why should these items be any different from your normal summer wardrobe? Well, if your destination is tropical, you will find that the light is different, and the sunshine is bright – what looks good in the city does not look good in Barbados or Mexico. Discard your navy, grey and black and go for colour and dazzling white. This is your opportunity to indulge in patterns and gauzy materials. Take along a white linen wrap-around skirt and add a loose, lime-green tunic with flat gold slides or platform sandals, a straw hat and sunglasses. Cheap cotton espadrilles would also do well, along with plastic, antique ivory or wooden jewellery.

Linen is best in hot climates because it acts like a walking air-condi-tioner. Shi on Lowndes Street, London, stocks a lovely linen "cruise col-lection" that includes Eastern-inspired flowing tunics, trousers, caftans and long skirts.

For dressier occasions we love the look of a sleeveless, knitted silk sweater with a below-the-knee chiffon skirt printed with little motifs. Add a matching cardigan, a loosely woven linen shawl and some mid- or high-heeled bronze or silver sandals. This simple look will take you to a party, restaurant or barbecue beach supper.

Invest in a pair of white linen drawstring trousers. If your figure permits, tie them slightly below the waist for a bit of 'edge'. Wear them by day over a bathing suit with rubber flip flops, or by night with a cropped camisole or T-shirt. Add some turquoise or coral beads, a matching bracelet and a colourful pashmina for those chillier moments in the evening.

Great Occasions

How we loathe occasion dressing. It is not that we hate weddings, bar mitzvahs, church fêtes, Ascot and Goodwood, but shelling out a fortune for an outfit of limited use sends us into deep depression. Is there any way to avoid having to traipse from shop to shop to find this mythical outfit? Is there something out there to set you off like a jewel amongst others? There is no easy answer.

If your daughter is getting married, we know it can be an unlimited palaver, but there are any number of good designers who can provide expert experience and advice – at a price. If you know that you have a number of functions to attend during the year, we encourage you to set out well ahead of the season and plan your wardrobe like a campaign for war. The best way to deal with the events calendar, whatever it may portend, is to have an Early Warning System. Write lists and devise combinations that serve two or three functions. For example, that new turquoise patent-leather clutch-bag goes with a black cocktail dress (already in your wardrobe) as well as with the jolly multicoloured caftan you wear every summer with the white trousers. A new, cream straw hat will double up at a country wedding as well as on the Florida beach later in the spring. Your perfectly plain, grey trouser-suit works for business, but can also serve for the Race Meeting at Ascot, teamed with high-heeled shoes, a lacy silk blouse and great piece of costume jewellery. Do not forget that hat. Fashion is a jigsaw puzzle.

If you really have nothing in the wardrobe, only then is it time to make an investment. Rather than going out and piecing an outfit together, arm yourself with some photographs of looks that you like and take these along with you to the boutiques you visit. Resist making your first purchase those tempting purple lizard, sling-back shoes because you will have to search the whole city before you find anything that looks good with them.

Even if you are a model size 8 or 10, you will have trouble locating special-occasion clothes (unless you started your search very early on in the season). This situation is only magnified for the less-than-perfect woman, who, if she leaves things to the last minute, will have to enter the Third Circle of Hell before she finds something appropriate. Fashion editors always seem to suggest that a larger lady should head for the High Street, as if this were some sort of magical place, and recommend that she wear the busiest patterns stampeding across the most ill-fitting of garments, forgetting that she is a person and has feelings.

The key to looking good for any occasion is, first and foremost, *relax*. Remember, you look happier when you are comfortable in your clothes. Most of us look better in two pieces because they fit well, and give us physical and mental flexibility. Unless a dress is designed and executed beautifully, with no lumps or bumps, it can look cheap and shapeless (and is so demanding). It does nothing for you, and its formality is ageing.

We are not suggesting that you give up that little black dress. But do think about breaking things up and persuading yourself to consider the virtues of a suit. A strict jacket over a soft-looking skirt or dress looks modern and relaxed, not rigid or fussy, which are banners for the elderly. Dive into your accessories drawer and pull out scarves, beads, belts and feathers. Apply, but restrict yourself to just one thing at a time. The French call this softness of dress a bit of '*flou*'. We call it movement. We prefer the look of a body-skimming, lacy suit to a dress that requires a host of special underwear effects. We like a long tunic and chain belt at the hips, over a knee-length pencil skirt. We admire the seemingly effortless Jackie O look of a silk tweed coat and matching shift dress. It was a winner in the 1960s and a retro look that is still good for us now.

While not wishing to play favourites, here are a few designers who we think do a good line in "occasion clothes."

Caroline Charles is a clever designer who makes great suits. For the summer she creates pieces with pretty pastels and for winter, rich velvets, brocades and tweeds. She puts elements together in an imaginative way and offers faux jewels and fake-fur boas as extras, to spice things up. Her separates work for both small and large sizes. Perhaps she succeeds because she is a working woman herself and understands a woman's needs, adapting current trends to her own, feminine vision.

Paddy Campbell is another great source of occasion dressing. Her pieces are always well made, coordinated (saving you the trouble) and classic. She features dresses with matching jackets or coats, often in wool crepe, with silk detailing to modernize and soften the edges.

Shayesteh Nazemi Shi, of cashmere fame, works wonders with magnificent Indian embroidered silks and taffetas. Her Shi label marries Persian sensibilities with a Western outlook in an intriguing way. Her one-size skirts and trousers, with drawstring or elasticated waists, work on a number of body types. If they are too ample, she will take them in; if they are too small, her workrooms will produce the correct size for your measurements. Her sweaters range from fitted to loose and long pieces with dolman sleeves. She has an eye for subtle colours and shading, which makes her clothes very flattering.

Yvonne Damant in Richmond, Surrey, is an innovative designer who specializes in dressy clothes for weddings and other events. Working in luxurious fabrics, she makes pieces that have a cutting edge. Her trousers are beautifully cut with proper waistbands, and she has a flair for the eccentric – her combat trousers are made for evenings in a rich, heavy black satin and adorned with a quirky khaki-coloured cord belt – in materials that are wonderfully opposing but work together. She also produces silk dresses in jewel-like colours, palazzo pants, embroidered and beaded coats, lightweight jackets and paste-studded belts accompanied by a range of antique costume jewellery.

A Short Word On Hats

European and British women wear hats to weddings, the races, royal events, garden parties and funerals – at least, some do. It is no longer an obligation but an option. In the 1960s, that great style icon, Jackie Kennedy, sported a bouffant hairdo styled by the famous Kenneth. To keep its volume intact she insisted on wearing a hat at the back of her head. She preferred simple felt or straw toques and eschewed the flowers and feathers of the previous generation. Hats implied status and traditional power, and in the young Kennedy administration, old conventions were cast away, which no doubt contributed to the demise of the hat's importance in the United States and the reduction in its size everywhere.

Today, hats are no longer regarded as the culmination of an elegant outfit, but they do remain a fashion choice. They add fun or eccentricity to any ensemble, but they can also be an encumbrance. It depends on who, where and what mood you're in. They are forever useful in the dead of winter for warmth – scientists tell us that a high percent of our body heat is lost through our heads – and in summer to shield us from the sun.

Nevertheless, there are few things that are as flattering on a woman as a beautiful hat. Conversely, an inappropriate hat can be ageing, recherché and the most dated item ever. The trick is to wear a hat because you want to. With a tailored suit, it is completely retro – almost a period costume, so out of date that it might even be deemed positively rebellious and cutting edge. Only someone like the late Isabella Blow, who was renowned for her eccentric hat collection made by her milliner-friend, Philip Treacy, could get away with it. Worn with jeans and a long, loose coat, flat shoes and sculptural jewellery, it could be a cool, modern and powerful individual statement. Good for art galleries. At a resort, a wide-brimmed straw hat is ubiquitous (and essential for health reasons). Furry hats are sexy and very Dr Zhivago. Worn with boots and a long, fitted Russophile coat, this would be chic on the streets of Paris, Milan or New York – but not London. (Be careful of old fur hats because they can appear dated and shabby. Proportions change imperceptibly over the years and what was once smart is devastatingly dated today.)

It is difficult to recommend a great hat maker because they are often private, bespoke designers, but the following are all good: Philip Treacy for his wit, Gabriella Ligenza for her feminine classicism and Basia Zarzycka for her over-the-top glamour. Caroline Charles has a nice selection of reasonably priced hats for all seasons. Department stores, such as Harrods, Harvey Nichols and Peter Jones in London, are also good sources where you can find a wide spectrum of prices and styles if you're prepared to spend time trying them all on. If you have a particular outfit in mind, take along a small sample of fabric or thread for colour matching.

Look for a good simple shape, not too severe, in a neutral colour – not so large that it would knock out someone's eye but something with style and presence. Stay away from cheap hats with too much trim. Huge ribbons are demanding but feathers can be fun. Remember that less is more. Veils can be a retro touch as long as you do not take yourself too seriously. Watch the red lipstick.

English weddings have their own rules, and there is a kind of shocking amusement when you witness the types and varieties of hat that are dragged out for the occasion. Almost invariably, they are "vintage," having been worn many times for the purpose. They can be enormous, blinding in fact, and are most likely hideous. But these hats are not intended to be smart. They are tribal, atavistic and not about fashion at all.

Working Women of a
Certain Age

What is a working woman's wardrobe? The average working mother might be a school administrator and have to dress appropriately every day for the office, meetings and conferences. If asked what her wardrobe consists of, she is likely to say, whatever reasonable thing she could find. Put simply, she doesn't have many choices. She claims that she could not wear trousers because they were not considered serious enough, and dresses did not suit her. Like many women over fifty, her shape was not perfectly proportioned, being smaller on top than on bottom. What might she want to look like? Her answer would echo any of our own responses: feminine, attractive and youthful without being overtly sexual. She wants respect in her job and to be taken seriously.

Many mature, professional women share these aspirations. But fashion designers, on the whole, do not cater to the seriousness or the flexibility that working women need. Men are lucky because suits, even if formal, is all they wear, save minor adjustments to the colour of their shirts and ties. Professional women desire the same ease of dress without being boring. They need to make the transition from boardroom to dining room with little time in between (not to mention packing space if they travel). Women complain that there is not enough choice, and the range of suits is uninspiring, cut in unflattering shapes with fabrics that are too masculine and unimaginative.

We see professional working women every day on planes and trains, grabbing their meals on the run, balancing mobiles between their chins and wrists while attempting to deal with their son's unexpected split with his girlfriend – and dressed, of course, in the ubiquitous grey flannel, shapeless suit with thick-soled sensible shoes and heavy-gauge nylon tights. This is the real story, not the *Sex and the City* version that features a glamorous woman lawyer on her way to court. The average career women is not racing for a train in her Manolo Blahnik's, nor is she uplifted, courtesy of Wonderbra, in her chiffon blouse. The real woman is commuting between home and office, city and suburb, immersed in paperwork and trying her hardest not to be overwhelmed by fatigue or looking dishevelled when she arrives for her meeting. She is not wearing silk combat trousers and a clingy, singlet top (unless she is chairing a conference on karate). She appears buttoned up and practical.

It *is* possible to escape the monotony of navy-blue, black, grey, brown and neutrals, but how do you add interest to your look without sending out counter-productive messages? Work is not only about your devotion to your job, it is about earning money. If you appear overly prosperous, your need to succeed might be brought into question. You do not want to look more expensively dressed than your boss or your client, but bad tailoring and plastic jewellery is not the answer either. Too many complicated accessories can confuse your message. You want to look smart and capable with womanly charm.

What can the professional woman do to smarten herself up without drawing too much attention to her clothes, instead of her work? First, accessories: belts, scarves, jewellery, makeup and bags should all be used, just like the non-career woman, only less. Second, identify the designers who create conservative pieces but with a bit of a twist. If you visit a department store, look at the clothing by Armani, Belvert, Krizia, Agnona, Max Mara, Rena Lange, Jil Sander, Strenesse and Celine – not cheap, but we are talking about an investment. The suit will be well cut, well made and a bit different from everyone else. Some women swear by Ferragamo's collection, with its emphasis on fine tailoring, classic handbags and shoes. With some effort, you could find the same look in a less expensive price range at Jaegar, Aquascutum, Daks, Viyella and Joseph.

Have business suits and skirts tailored closer to your body. Long jackets are flattering if you are a bit hippy, but it is better to have some indication of a waist. Short jackets work if you are heavier on top than on bottom. A light-coloured jacket on the top with a darker skirt minimizes the hips and bottom. A short jacket with a bias-cut skirt minimizes the hips as well, and its fluted lines emphasize ankles. A darker jacket above a lighter bottom-half emphasizes a narrower waist. Bear these proportions in mind when you are trying suits on, and get the tailor to pin any excess material for a more body-skimming fit. A centimetre or two can transform something a bit dumpy into something svelte and chic.

A useful alternative is a dress with matching coat or jacket. It is elegant, useful and can be recombined in a number of ways. The coat can be worn with numerous other outfits, the jacket may go with trousers and a pullover, and the dress can take you into the evening, especially if you add a pretty shawl and accent with jewellery. Although you will not want to wear a very short skirt, opt for the pencil variety (if you are heavy of hip), which stops at the knee or is no more than a half-inch below. Not a mini, not a micro, but with a tiny indication that you have legs and you like them. A-line skirts hide many flaws, as long as the accompanying jacket is short and curvy, but ensure that it does not fall much below the knee or it can look frumpy. In our experience, long, straight skirts worn with mid-heel shoes are neither attractive, feminine nor a good disguise. If you prefer skirts mid-calf, wear boots and a long-fitted cardigan in the same colour, rather than a jacket. It will take years and pounds off your look. Add a belt if you have a good waist, put a T-shirt underneath with a little silver necklace and wear a cape or scarf. This look is conservative but fashionable and slightly different. Try variations on the theme, and apply to your summer wardrobe with lighter fabrics.

Blouses are an instant formula for dressing things up and creating an elegant, lady-like impression. Chiffon and silk are lovely because they suggest a hint of flesh underneath, without being conspicuous. If they are too see-through, buy a cotton or silk undervest by Hanro. Although we love neat little sweaters, T-shirts and bare skin under jackets, for the working woman a pretty soft pastel, off-white or black silky blouse is better. It looks professional and correct during the day, and can be dressed up for evening with a bit of extra makeup and jewellery.

Avoid like the plague the thing called the "body," invented by Donna Karan in the 1970s. It seemed like such a revolutionary idea at the time, a snug, low-necked top that fastened under the crotch. The intention was smoothness, neatness and practicality. What could be more useful? An iron maiden or a truss? They are uncomfortable, get soiled fast and make bulges on the sides. They flatten the bosom and push out your underarm flab (which you had not noticed until then) in the most alarming manner. It is a no-go item after thirty-five, maybe earlier.

By all means wear shoes that you can walk in comfortably. Very high heels are tiring, so opt for a lower, slimmer heel with a low throat. Try sling-back or kitten-heeled suede boots. There is something about the "cover-up factor" that indicates extra sex appeal. Stay away from anything that smacks of being butch – no heavy Dr Martens or motorcycle boots, unless you are working for Harley Davidson. Invest in a pair of rainproof, Gore-Tex ankle boots for bad weather; they are neat, feminine and practical. If you must wear the highest heels, in the palest buttery-smooth leather, take them to work in a carrier bag and restrict yourself to wearing them at your desk. These are not designed for public transport, or endless pacing up and down corridors.

Earrings are authoritative. Why? Just take our word for it. For work, however, they have to be button earrings, close to the face, not the size of dinner plates, and in good colours. Avoid anything too dangling or sparkling in the office, although if you work in an art gallery or are a psychiatrist, speech therapist or professor of aerodynamics, feel free to be more adventurous in this department. Adding focus to any outfit and pulling your look together, earrings are good for lawyers, doctors, bankers and business consultants and a finishing touch that says 'Take Me Seriously'. Be careful with modern clip-on earrings (the gold swirls, the pearls pasted onto circular backings, the single gemstone-studs), which can look boring, predictable and say very little about you. Wean yourself off popular models and go for something antique. The latter will always say 'I Am Unique' and can be surprisingly affordable (see the chapter on jewellery).

Brooches, bracelets and pearls are serious. Neat, gold necklaces and chokers are serious. A good-looking watch is serious. Just remember that for work, every detail needs to be kept in proportion. Discretion is everything, so save the big, chunky stuff and vintage plastic for the weekend.

Working women can wear colour, but avoid too much of it in a single dose. Although many of us are drawn to the bright red suit, a red jacket matched with a grey or tobacco coloured skirt is a better idea (less airline hostess). Red is a powerful, stimulating colour, and can be worn in all kinds of fabrics – tweed, gabardine, suede, leather and velvet in shades ranging from deepest carnelian to tomato. Although we are all devoted to black (a rational choice with red), other hues such as tan, navy and grey are softer and more chic. Coordinate with antique pearl jewellery for a striking look. Bright Gitane-blue can be difficult to wear except by the palest blondes or darkest brunettes; a paler blue is prettier. As a well-tailored Agnona blazer, it is positively dressy but less severe. We love pastels, such as pale pink and chartreuse, for the summer. Team up your "pales" with a dark suit and you will transform the look. Stay away from grassy greens unless you are in Palm Beach, or fluorescent lime colours except when sipping pinot grigio in Forte dei Marmi. Go for olive and sludgier tones if you are "green."

Tweeds are always in for business or for play, but other loud patterns are best left for holidays. Try a neat tweed jacket with a brown leather skirt, and add some Scottish agate jewellery – a pair of small shield-shaped earrings, a brooch or bracelet. This is a great look and will not be seen on anyone else. Knitted suits can be comfortable and useful for travel, but they must be well fitted – not baggy in the bottom or mis-shapen (which tends to happen over time). There is nothing worse than a saggy back-end view of a woman in a knitted or jersey suit. St John's, a brand much loved by America's middle-aged set, specialize in these easy-wear pieces, but we think they can look plastic and elderly. Elasti-cated waists, big gilt buttons and fussy bows can add at least ten years to your age.

Our sympathies lie with the working woman. Your difficult juggling act is always to be admired, but your lack of fashion choice (at affordable prices) seems so punishing. Until we get better designers who can focus on the real needs of career women, the future looks pretty dismal. Do the best you can by using what is out there and making it your own. Remember: tailors are your friends, accessorize and smile.

CHAPTER THIRTY-TWO

Finally...

It might be a gross generalization to say that all of us yearn for style. Indeed, you may be one of those rare women for whom glamour is an irrelevance, an interference with life's other passions. For many of us, however, the way we look and feel about ourselves is an ongoing concern. You may sculpt like Brancusi, or plant herbaceous borders like Vita Sackville-West, but your creativity can flourish with a bit of eyeliner.

Cultural and financial restraints need not hold you back. A woman in her chador may well be catering to her sense of femininity by wearing frilly knickers and a silky caftan underneath those sombre robes. The mother whizzing down the supermarket aisles in her velour tracksuit can still choose to wear a lacy satin camisole if it makes her feel better. The divorcée with two problem teenagers and an inadequate cash settlement can still crave the look and feel of a Prada cardigan.

For those on tighter budgets the problems begin with the High Street. Window after shop window reveal the same old uninspired, poorly made garments. Middle-aged women in the middle market are confronted with indifferently designed frumpy skirts, shapeless sweaters and dresses, boring twin-sets and baggy trousers. This year's styles seem to be passing you by. Clothes appear in garish or dreary colours. The 'look' prescribed for the 'maturer' woman may be faintly ethnic, sporty or schoolmarmish, but you emerge looking either like a refugee from *Far Pavilions* or a contestant on *The Weakest Link*.

On the same street there are also the blatantly sexual, tarty styles: satin push-up bra dresses, the tightest hipster trousers, see-through fabrics smothered in sequins and corseted jackets that pinch and bind. These are clothes for teenagers on the make, neither elegant nor flattering on adult women. There are the knock-off artists, such as Zara, Karen Millen and Topshop, not to mention all the Chanel-style lookalikes in every price range. Some of these copies, however, are poorly made, compromised in their design integrity and, worse, expensive for what they are.

We believe it is possible to achieve style on less than an oligarch's income if you know the market, what is fashionable and right for you. Ten final thoughts:

1. Use this book as an inspiration. You do not need to shop at the best boutiques and department stores but visit them to inform yourself of what is quality, beautiful and contemporary. Wander through the hallowed halls of Chanel, Armani, Valentino and others. Ignore the vacant stares of the black-suited doormen, look at the clothes and take your time – feel them, try them on to get an idea of the workmanship and fit. Do not feel intimidated: no one need know that you have no intention of actually making a purchase.

2. Do your research. You must flick through the pages of the fashion magazines and newspapers every week, and scan the advertisements and pictures for what is in vogue. There is no need to read the articles, but peruse the images so that you can derive their essence. Without research, you will not know how things go together for a "style update."

3. Love what you buy and look after it. Try to protect your treasured item, especially if you paid a lot for it. Do not sleep on planes and trains in your good clothes. Air them out once you have worn them for a few hours instead of shoving them back into drawers and cupboards. Avoid dry-cleaning too often, and keep a practical eye on what you will be doing that day or evening to avoid accidents – a silk blouse with voluminous sleeves and dangling bow at the neck may be pretty but not the best choice for a slap-up Chinese meal.

4. Remember that accessories work hard and are crucial for getting your image right, especially on a limited budget. A great belt, terrific handbag or beautiful gloves can transform something ordinary into something truly elegant. Given the choice between yet another plain black cardigan costing £75 from the High Street and a silky twirl of a scarf by Missoni with the same price tag, always go for the latter. This is what a classic is: an investment in style that will serve you well over time.

5. You may have heard of *Bon Chic Bon Genre*, a catchphrase that embraces a whole way of life. It is something to aspire to and remains as relevant today as it was in our mothers' generation. The secret, as always, was and is *in the fit*. Get that right and anything you buy is brought up to a new and improved standard. A proper fit will extend a garment's life because